REMEMBER

the *why*

M000032141

REMEMBER
the
why

WHY FOLLOWING JESUS MAKES SENSE
(EVEN WHEN EVERYTHING FEELS BROKEN)

LINDSEA PATTISON

ILLUMIFY
MEDIA.COM

REMEMBER
the
why

Copyright © 2021 by Lindsea Pattison
All rights reserved. No part of this book may be reproduced in any form or by any means—
whether electronic, digital, mechanical, or otherwise—without permission in writing from
the publisher, except by a reviewer, who may quote brief passages in a review.

All Scripture quotations are taken from THE HOLY BIBLE, NEW INTERNATIONAL
VERSION®, NIV®. Copyright © 1973, 1978, 1984, 2011 by Biblica, Inc.® All rights
reserved worldwide.

The views and opinions expressed in this book are those of the author and do not necessarily
reflect the official policy or position of Illumify Media Global.

Published by
Illumify Media Global
www.IllumifyMedia.com
"Let's bring your book to life!"

Library of Congress Control Number: 2021922484

Paperback ISBN: 978-1-955043-42-7

Typeset by Art Innovations (http://artinnovations.in/)
Cover design by Debbie Lewis

Printed in the United States of America

DEDICATION

To all of my girls, who remind me why I started.
To my future self. Girl, you did it!
To everyone reading this who feels frustrated, hurt, broken, and
lost. You are not alone. You are loved.
To my family, thank you for inspiring me to be the strong woman
I am today. I love you all so much.

Remind yourself why you started pursuing Jesus in the first place and why your purpose in this world is worth fighting for. Begin the journey of transformation by working against bitterness, frustration, and heartbreak, then learn to love Jesus and yourself.

CONTENTS

Acknowledgements   ix

Introduction   xi

1. The Yellow Butterfly   1
2. One True Love   18
3. Fighting the Good Fight   38
4. Choose Joy   51
5. The Bigger Picture   62
6. Looking in the Mirror   82
7. The Power of Your Tongue   99
8. Gut Feelings   110
9. This World Is Broken   122
10. Social Media   135
11. Renewing the Mind   147
12. Surrendering Control   156
13. All About Jesus   167
14. Life Changes   193
15. Then There Was Another Butterfly   209

About the Author   224

ACKNOWLEDGEMENTS

For all of my girls. You know who you are. You have inspired me to become the woman I am today and to write this book from start to finish. Don't give up, queens. You are so loved.

Let me give a special shout-out to my cousin, Tessa. Never give up on yourself, on your relationship with Jesus, or on others. You are beautiful, and I am so proud of the woman you are becoming.

Thank you to all the people who were there when I was falling and who picked me back up. To my roomies of "The Honeycomb." You always offered shoulders to ugly cry on and reminded me of the truths about Jesus. To my *three* roommates of "Good ole RV." Thank you for pushing me toward Jesus when I needed him the most. Thank you for the knowledge and love you have brought me and for showing me what it means to have godly relationships.

Thank you to my hype-up girls: Chelsea, Maddie, Caroline, Rachel, Skylar, Addison, Leigh, and Macie. Your continuous support and your reminders to love myself have improved my life greatly. You all truly deserve the world.

Thank you to all of my leaders and mentors throughout my high school and college experience. You know who you are! The amount of love and support my friends and family have given me throughout this process has been outstanding.

Thank you to all of you who loved me when I was the most stubborn human being, when I procrastinated, and when I didn't think I was worth it. Thank you for standing next to me and holding my hand every step of the way.

Thank you to all of those women who reminded me to love Jesus and to not look back. ***The journey has just begun.***

INTRODUCTION

*A*t the beginning of my senior year in college, I felt frustrated, disillusioned, and unseen.

For three years I had been involved in a campus ministry. I'd even served in a leadership role. But I felt empty. I felt unseen from the beginning. Over three years, I was never asked to share my testimony with anyone, which lead me to believe this lie: my story wasn't worth sharing.

I wasn't a favorite among this group, or so I thought.

One night, I was worshipping at a young adults' gathering at Red Rocks Church in Littleton, Colorado. In a quiet moment, I heard God whispering to me: *Write a book.* I questioned it at first because not only was it super random—I thought it was impossible.

Me? Write a book?

As the fall semester continued, however, my faith took a hit. I was slammed with frustration and doubt. I sensed favoritism toward certain people who were in the campus ministry, and I always felt like I was stepping on eggshells around Christians. I felt lost and broken, and I soon forgot all of the reasons why I was following Jesus.

Not long after the experience at Red Rocks Church, I left the campus ministry and soon fell into old patterns of sin. I started frequenting bars and getting drunk. I felt judged and alone. And knowing what the Bible says about my choices hurt me even more. I felt like an outcast.

But a small thought kept nagging at me: *Write a book.*

And so, I did.

I wrote this book for four reasons:

1. I needed to remind myself *why* I had followed Jesus in the first place, why parts of my faith were important to me, and why (despite setbacks) I really *was* committed to following him to the end.

2. I wanted to fall in love with Jesus all over again.

3. I wanted to encourage others to do the same.

4. I felt that God asked me to write this book.

Remember the Why was inspired by my frustration, by the fact that I almost gave up, and by how close I came to forgetting why I pursued Jesus in the first place.

There are always going to be frustrations within the church, ministries, and youth groups. Working through these frustrations with Jesus allowed me to get to the place where I am today.

This book is a reminder that while people are imperfect, Jesus is perfect. He is good, he is just, and he has a plan for you despite your frustrations, pains, and hurts. In fact, he can even use them for his glory! This life can get screwed up. It's easy to forget that God really does have a plan and purpose for us as Christians in this world.

As I was thinking about writing this book, I got more involved with my church in Fort Collins. I served in the kids' ministry and on the creative team, which allowed me to take some small steps back toward Jesus. All the while, though, I was still going to bars and living in sin.

In this process, God was gently waiting for me to run back to him.

James 4:13–17 encouraged me throughout this whole process of writing this book:

> "Now listen, you who say, 'Today or tomorrow we will go to this or that city, spend a year there, carry on business and make money.' Why, you do not even know what will happen tomorrow. What is your life? You are a mist that appears for a little while and then vanishes. Instead, you ought to say, 'If it is the Lord's will, we will live and do this or that.' As it is, you boast in your arrogant schemes. All such boasting is evil. If anyone, then, knows the good they ought to do and doesn't do it, it is sin for them."

I had tried to plan my life out. I had wanted to do my own thing. And when I realized I couldn't do it on my own, Jesus continued fighting for me. He directed me to believe his truths and to the roots of the lies I was believing about myself.

I need Jesus. I need the power of the Holy Spirit. I need God's grace and truths.

And whether or not you realize it fully right now, so do you. I hope this book encourages you to fall more in love with Jesus every day of your life.

"I pray that out of his glorious riches he may strengthen you with power through his Spirit in your inner being, so that Christ may dwell in your hearts through faith. And I pray that you, being rooted and established in love, may have power, together, with all the Lord's holy people, to grasp how wide and long and high and deep in the love of Christ, and to know his love that surpasses knowledge-that you may be filled to the measure of all the fullness of God." (Ephesians 3:16-19)

CHAPTER 1

THE YELLOW BUTTERFLY
Why Are the Power of Testimonies Important?

*I*t all started when a yellow butterfly hit me right in the nose in the parking lot of my grandma's nursing home. It was at the end of my freshman year of college, and I wasn't in a good place. Here's why:

- I was in a relationship with an unstable, mentally abusive guy from high school.
- I was drinking, smoking, and taking Adderall that was not prescribed to me.
- I was battling anxiety, pain, and darkness.

Every day I prayed for happiness and for God to help me get out of situations I had put myself in. During this time, I was reading the book *To Heaven and Back*, in which the author points out that God communicates in different ways, often using animals and nature to speak into people's lives.

So there I was, sitting in my car in the parking lot of my grandma's nursing home, praying for freedom, change, and even a small measure of happiness. The night before, I had slept with my boyfriend again—in fact, I had just come from his house—and shame continued to eat at me.

When I stepped out of my car, a huge monarch butterfly immediately flew into my face. I could feel its wings on my nose. The experience was so intriguing, I decided to Google what a butterfly symbolizes.

I learned that "the butterfly is a symbol of change, joy, and color." And since it was a yellow butterfly, my search regarding color suggested words like "sunshine, hope, and happiness."

After praying for freedom, happiness, and change in my situation, I knew God was trying to tell me something.

And his messages to me didn't end there.

After visiting with my grandma and telling her what had just happened, I got in my car and turned on the local Christian radio station, K-Love. The radio host was talking about freedom and letting go of things that you are holding on to. I felt a sense of shock at how everything was aligning with what I felt God was saying to me.

Could this really be happening? Was God really speaking to me?

Apparently, God knew I was going to raise that question and was already working on his response.

As I was doubting and driving home, I passed a huge billboard that had a picture of a yellow butterfly and the words "New Friends." Flabbergasted, I pulled into the parking lot of the apartment building where I lived in the summer of 2017 with my sister and my mom. Immediately, I searched for my sister to tell her what had happened. I found her lounging at the pool.

While I was telling her the story of the monarch butterfly and the billboard butterfly, two small yellow butterflies flew by us.

I'm not kidding.

I was so taken aback by this experience that I pulled my journal from my backpack and began scribbling down what was happening. My sister, however, wasn't impressed. She had her doubts.

At that moment, yet another yellow monarch butterfly flew right in front of both of us. My sister and I both gasped, and I felt a rush of the Holy Spirit course through me.

I knew exactly what God was trying to tell me, and I decided to listen to him. I was determined to surrender every part of my life completely to Jesus in obedience. I got rid of all of my toxic relationships—including my mentally abusive boyfriend—and made the decision right then to be all in with Jesus.

Flash-forward a couple of months later, when I started my sophomore year of college.

I found amazing friendships and connections.

I experienced more happiness than ever before.

God brought me contentment and endless joy.

I started to value day-to-day life and appreciate the wonder of all that God has created.

One day, I went on a run in City Park in Fort Collins, Colorado. While running—and feeling as joyful and content as ever—a yellow monarch butterfly flew right in front of me. Yes, *again*!

At that moment, I knew God was saying, *I told you so.*

OUR STORIES GLORIFY GOD

Now I've shared with you my story, or at least part of it. It matters when we share our stories with each other for many reasons. When we tell our God-stories, we give glory to God. When we tell our God-stories, we impact the lives of our listeners and readers. God speaks to other people through our stories so they can be encouraged. When we tell our God-stories, we also encourage ourselves and build up our own faith. Life is busy, and it's easy for us to get distracted and forget the many ways God has already intervened in our lives. Telling our stories keeps these memories fresh—and our faith strong.

And that's why testimonies are powerful.

The truth is, your story matters. Your mess matters. You matter.

I want to make space for your story for a moment. Let me ask you a few questions. I'm going to put them here, and—if you turn to the end of this chapter—you'll find the same questions with space for you to respond:

- Are you following Jesus? If not, what is holding you back? If yes, why did you start following Jesus? Recall your earliest memory.
- When did you fully give your life to Jesus?
- What did you feel like when you let go of control?
- Why did you feel like you needed to give your life to Jesus?
- What did your life look like before Jesus entered it?

My journey with Jesus began when I was pretty young. My mom told me, "God loves you so much that he sent Jesus down to die on the cross and save you from your sins and wants to spend eternity with you. All you have to do is accept the grace he has given you and follow him." At that moment, I believed in Jesus because of his truth. I felt his love and I wanted to spend the rest of my life knowing his love. Then she prayed with me. At that moment, my faith felt instantly stronger, and the Holy Spirit rushed into my being as I accepted him in my heart. Now, I wish every moment was like that one. I wish my faith today was as easy to tap into as it was when I was a little kid.

Then again, why does it have to be harder? Perhaps we can draw lessons from our childhood experiences with faith. As children, we don't handle all the responsibilities in our lives. Instead, we relax and let our parents handle things for us.

Can we do the same with God? What if we let go of all of our burdens and problems and gave them to God every day? What if we truly held on to Jesus and his truths just like we hold on to our parents' hands when there's trouble? The unwillingness to bring your feelings to God keeps you in denial and stops you from being in reality. When was the last time you gave your feelings to God? Express your anger, sorrow & fear to God.

Jesus worked throughout my broken, imperfect story and continued to guide me to him. I look back on my story, and I can't help but smile because I have seen him work to get me where I am today: filled with the Holy Spirit and trusting Jesus to use my story to bring others to redemption.

OUR STORIES INCLUDE OUR VICTORIES AND OUR FAILURES

In my sophomore year of high school, I attended a Christian camp in Sedalia, Colorado, called NYR (National Youth Roundup). I remember a pastor on stage saying, "If your relationship ends, if your parents get divorced, or if your grandma dies, Jesus is still the same today, yesterday, and forever."

Not long after that, my high school boyfriend and I broke up, and my parents went through a nasty divorce. Luckily, my grandma is still alive and healthy. But when that time comes, I know that I am going to be okay because I can hold onto Jesus.

When I was in high school, little did I know that my journey with Jesus was just beginning. I volunteered and was a mentor to younger girls in church. But that's not where my story lives. My full story was crafted in the rough moments at home, at my high school boyfriend's house, and through my insecurities.

I mentioned that my parents went through a nasty divorce. About that time, I was in a four-year relationship with a boy. His family helped me get through a lot of awful things at home. However, I also fell into a lot of sin with him. I wasn't the girl I wanted to be when I was dating him. In fact, I didn't like any part of myself in high school. The boy I was dating was consumed with video games, much like any other high school boy; therefore, he couldn't meet many of my relational needs because he was often "checked out" in a fantasy world.

All that to say, I kept trying to grab hold of something other than Jesus to fulfill my worth and my needs. And guess what? It only led me to discontentment and allowed me to feel even more insecure and unworthy. Because of this, I ran toward another boy who was giving me attention, and I ended up cheating on my high school boyfriend. It took me about six years to forgive myself for that mistake. I was left with painful questions and thoughts:

Why did I cheat?
I am worthless.
I am unworthy.

I know now that was the devil talking to me, speaking lies into my soul. Over time, though, I realized that I am more than the choices that I made. It's what I did, not who I am. The kingdom of God is about accepting his love and knowing we are washed by the blood of Christ. This means that he washed us clean by his sacrifice. Likewise, your choices you made isn't who you are. Because of what Jesus did, we are renewed by his blood.

Don't waste valuable years believing Satan's lies. What we need to remind ourselves is that Jesus forgives us. Jesus is our Redeemer. Jesus defines us. The truth sets us free. Romans 6:15-16 says "What then? Shall we sin because we are not under the law but under grace? By no means! Don't you know that when you offer yourselves to someone as obedient slaves, you are slaves of the one you obey—whether you are slaves to sin, which leads to death, or to obedience, which leads to righteousness?"

Our mistakes are an important part of our stories. As we share the truth—which is that we all sin and fall short of the glory of God—it brings others to Jesus, brings us new life, and brings others new life.

How amazing is *that*? God can use my broken, messed-up story to lead others to Jesus and to heaven. He can use it to renew people's lives here on earth. And he will use your story, too, if you accept his forgiveness and let him help you forgive yourself.

Our loving Jesus, chased after me the entire time in high school. He loved me the entire time, even when I was cheating and acting out in sin.

Looking back, I can see that Jesus was fighting for my attention, fighting for me to come back home, but I was too ashamed to come back to him. I thought I had messed up too much.

Then, I remembered that Jesus died for all of my sins and saved me. I remembered he didn't see me as my sins, he saw me as his beloved daughter.

I remembered that God is powerful enough to work in every chapter of my story.

OUR STORIES ENCOURAGE OTHERS

Right before COVID-19 shut down everything in 2020, I decided to lead a few Bible studies: one for my college girls and one for my high school girls. As my passion for leadership continued to develop, I knew it was God's plan in the making.

The college Bible study that I started was born out of my frustration with the campus ministry I had been involved in. What's amazing is that my experience was not uncommon. The more I interacted with other young women, the more I saw that they carried wounds similar to mine. Girls would share with me the same frustrations and hurts I had experienced that had driven them away from other ministries too.

During the Bible studies, I got to know these girls deeply, and share the love of Jesus with them.

Then, COVID-19 happened, and our Bible study got moved online.

But there was power in that too.

There was power in speaking into each other's lives, encouraging each other to continue to push through and wake up talking to Jesus each day—even if we were doing it through a screen.

My story of feeling broken and hurt helped the girls feel like they weren't alone in their feelings. I was able to relate to them because of the hardships I had gone through. The messed-up things in my life spoke to others and helped nudge them toward Jesus.

The other Bible study I started—the one for high school girls—was launched when God spoke to me unexpectedly. I was enjoying a run outdoors, where my mind could be free and receptive to God's natural wonders. It wasn't long before I felt God speak into my heart and instruct me to reach out to my younger cousin and ask if she would be interested in getting a group together to study the Bible. A week later, my aunt texted me that God had put on her heart the idea of me hosting a Bible study with my cousin and her friends. This was without her even knowing what God had told me, or that I had already reached out to my cousin.

I didn't think simply meeting with three high school girls every week would have the significant impact on my life and theirs as it did. Leading each of these girls into a deeper journey with Jesus ended up changing all of our lives.

Again, the stories of our journeys with Jesus have power.

Now, it's possible that you don't think you have a God-story yet. It's possible that you haven't begun *your* journey with Jesus. If so, I have some good news for you: You can start today! No matter where you have been, no matter the sin and brokenness you have experienced in your life, Jesus is waiting to forgive you and give you a brand-new life in him.

God sent his one and only son, Jesus, to die a painful death on the cross and become the ultimate sacrifice for you and for me. And when we accept that gift, we not only receive the promise of eternal life with God, we become a part of God's kingdom and family here on earth.

If you're ready to accept Jesus' gift and sacrifice, the one he made possible through his death upon the cross, I want you to know one thing: it's free. We don't need to work to spend eternity with God, we only have to repent and turn from our sins and trust Jesus. And the crazy part is, you can accept this gift from Jesus today, or whenever you are ready.

Get somewhere by yourself and begin to talk to Jesus. Tell him you're sorry for living your life without him. Tell him you want to have a relationship with him and you're ready to receive all that he made possible for you through his death on the cross. Open your heart, then listen for his response.

The apostle Paul states, "For the wages of sin is death, but the gift of God is eternal life in Christ Jesus our Lord" (Romans 6:23).

In the book of John, we are told, "For God so loved the world that he gave his one and only Son, that *whoever* believes in him shall not perish but have eternal life" (John 3:16, emphasis added).

The point is, you are *never* too far gone.

You are forgiven. You are loved. You can start a new life with Jesus today. And if you've had a relationship with him in the past and then let it waver, you can rekindle that relationship with Jesus and fall in love with him all over again. My friend Andrea has a powerful story about how she started following Jesus.

ANDREA'S STORY

Here are some quick facts about me: I am an only child. My mother is a believer. My father is not. They divorced when I was three. While I am thankful they both remain in my life, I endured a lot of pain, verbal abuse, conditional love, switching from house to house, and being placed in the middle of my parents' arguments. However, my situation gave me deep and interesting insight into what life looks like *with* Jesus (Mom), and what it looks like *without* him (Dad). Let me tell you, there is a huge difference!

While growing up, my faith was tied to my mom's faith, and I was "lukewarm" in my pursuit of Christ. I wasn't sure if I was ready, good enough, or confident enough to follow Jesus because I couldn't accept or understand that he was *actually* real and *actually* died for me. It just did not click. It wasn't until my sophomore year of college when I finally surrendered completely to God.

My transformation happened when I was at a Christian camp in the mountains of Colorado. During a worship gathering, we were singing the song "I Run to the Altar" by Bishop Noel Jones. I felt this overwhelming sense and pull that God wanted me to be fully committed, so I finally built up the courage to answer yes.

I didn't know what that meant. I didn't have all the answers. And I didn't understand completely what I was walking into. But I did know I was tired of living the lukewarm way: believing but not committing. It was a scary place to be, so I chose to be 100 percent in on the side of love, grace, sacrifice, mercy, goodness, righteousness, forgiveness, and so much more. I felt it in my bones that I was a creation and I had a Creator. I now follow Jesus because he is the hope and peace of the world, and the purest definition of love.

Throughout my journey with God, I have seen what restoration he can do. For example, I had a very broken relationship with my father, and by the grace of God, Jesus helped me forgive him (which was not easy), and now my relationship with my dad is better than it's ever been.

When I feel distant from God, anxious, or worried, I look at the beautiful world around me, how specifically created it is, and remind myself of Matthew 6:26: "Look at the birds of the air; they do not sow or reap or store away in barns, and yet your heavenly Father feeds them. Are you not much more valuable than they?" God sees you. He knows you. He wants a relationship with you. Believing in him, even if you do not have it all figured out, is all he asks for.

Learn more about Paul's testimony in the bible. Acts 9:1-19, Acts 13:9, Acts 16:16-40, Philippians 3:4-17

——————— REFLECTION QUESTIONS ———————

1. Why is it important to share your testimony?

2. Why is it important to remind yourself that your story matters?

3. What remarkable things has Jesus done in your life?

4. What are you feeling? Anger, sorrow, fear?

YOUR TURN

I promised earlier in this chapter that you would have space to begin writing your story. Answer these questions here to get started:

- Are you following Jesus? If not, what is holding you back? If yes, why did you start following Jesus? Recall your earliest memory.

- When did you fully give your life to Jesus?

- What did you feel when you let go of control?

- Why did you feel like you needed to give your life to Jesus?

- What did your life look like before Jesus entered it?

CHAPTER 2

ONE TRUE LOVE

Why Honor God in a Relationship and in Singleness?

When we put Jesus first in our relationships, it empowers us to love others and ourselves better.

When it comes to dating, I've screwed up plenty of times. For the longest time I didn't think I deserved a guy who followed Jesus wholeheartedly. Because of the mistakes in my past, I expected to date someone who would treat me poorly. I definitely didn't feel I deserved someone who measured up to the godly standards described in Job 31 or Proverbs 31. When I'd listen to my favorite podcasts hosted by Christian dating experts, I wondered how I would ever attract a godly man, as they described, if I didn't truly believe I was worthy of that

When we put Jesus first in our relationships, it empowers us to love others and ourselves better.

standard. I believed the lie that I had to find a relationship that made me happy when Jesus is the only one that will fulfill that need.

Here's what I know now: We don't *deserve* anything good. In fact, without the blood of Christ, we deserve hell. When sin entered the world in the book of Genesis, we became sinful. But when Jesus died for our sins, things changed.

Let me rephrase what I just said so it hits home: Jesus died for our messed-up, broken life and for our mistakes so that we might experience some of the joy and the life that God intended for us to live. Maybe I don't deserve that "amazing" and "perfect" guy. Maybe I don't even deserve a relationship at all. I definitely don't *deserve* salvation. But Jesus changed everything when he died on that cross. Now, we who claim him as our Lord are worthy. Through him, our worth is renewed.

Jesus forgives you. Jesus loves you despite your divorce, despite your multiple infidelities, and despite your frequent screw-ups. We don't need to strive to find a Godly relationship. We have a God that desires what's best for us. We are his children that he loves and cares for.

Jeremiah 29:11 says, "For I know the plans I have for you," declares the LORD, "plans to prosper you and not to harm you, plans to give you hope and a future."

No matter your age, God can restore you. He can turn your brokenness and your mistakes into healing and redemption. What a good and gracious God! Jesus comes first, and he is your one true love. His love story is the best love story you will ever experience. Once you find your one true love in him, you'll realize you don't need anything else. And yet God loves blessing us with gifts beyond our wildest dreams—even if it isn't what we expect.

When we put Jesus first in our relationships, it empowers us to love others and ourselves better. We become better equipped to love as Jesus loves, not by idolizing a person, but by building them up and giving them the grace that God has freely given to us.

On the flip side, sometimes loving someone means calling them out on their sins. This only happens after much prayer and relying on God. God is the ultimate judge (Isaiah 33:32), and calling each other out on sins isn't to bring shame or guilt. Its purpose is to bring people life, not death. Our job as followers of Jesus is to not judge each other but to love one another. This is highly misunderstood in the American culture. We need to desperately depend on Jesus and the gospel in this fallen world.

And as we seek God, he'll help us help others too:

Proverbs 19:20–21 states, "Listen to advice and accept discipline, and at the end you will be counted among the wise. Many are the plans in a person's heart, but it is the LORD's purpose that prevails."

Perhaps, at this point in your life, God hasn't brought what you expected. That's okay. Remember, he knit you together in your mother's womb; therefore, you can trust that he knows what is best for you. Be thankful for what you have now. There's always single people wanting to be married and there's always married people wanting to be single. Trust him for what you need tomorrow. Enjoy the friendships and connections you have with people, and consider them just as holy as a romantic relationship. You might have your version of ideal "plans," but trust me on this: God's ideal plans and purpose are much better. Be patient, then look back on the beautiful orchestrations later that brought you what you needed, when you needed it.

Romans 8:25–27 says, "But if we hope for what we do not yet have, we wait for it patiently. In the same way, the Spirit helps us in our weakness. We do not know what we ought to pray for, but the Spirit himself intercedes for us through wordless groans. And he who searches our hearts knows the mind of the Spirit, because the Spirit intercedes for God's people in accordance with the will of God."

This verse reminds me to pray for patience and pray for the endurance to await the things I desire and that God desires for me.

HONORING GOD MEANS WE DON'T HAVE TO SETTLE

I don't know if you were a huge Club Penguin fan as a kid, but I certainly was. If you're familiar with Club Penguin, my favorite game by far was ice fishing. If you're not familiar with the game, let me give you a quick summary.

The goal of this online, virtual-world game is to catch a big fish despite a bunch of obstacles—like random shoes and crabs—that can cut off your fishing line. One strategy is to have a small fish on your fishing line at all times. This allows you to catch a bigger fish by the end of the game.

As I got older, I thought of dating the same way.

I figured I always needed to have a small fish on the line if I were to have a chance at snagging a bigger fish.

That "small fish" was typically a guy I knew wasn't right for me, someone I had settled for in the hopes of trading him in at some point for someone better. I'd hang on to the small fish for the longest time because I wasn't trusting God in that area of my life. I wasn't trusting God to place the right man in my life; therefore, I clung to poor quality relationships.

What does it look like to trust God in this?

Recently, I completed a devotional about the love story of Ruth and Boaz. This is a real story about real people, it's not fictional. Here's what happened: Ruth's husband died, as well as her father-in-law and brother-in-law. One minute she was content in marriage, the other minute the worst-case scenario had unfolded. Her true love had died, and she was the only one left to take care of her mother-in-law, Naomi. Ruth worked hard from early morning to late at night to pay for rent and for food for herself and Naomi.

My favorite part of this true story is how Ruth's workplace ended up being a wheat field owned by her second future husband, Boaz.

Throughout the entire story, the owner of the field watched over Ruth and protected her. He did this out of brotherly love. He didn't have any hidden agenda. He only wanted to protect Ruth out of the kindness of his heart.

Boaz was well respected in the community. He was trustworthy. He was kind. In other words, he was a big fish worth waiting for.

What if Ruth had "filled her time" by settling for the wrong fish until the right fish came along? Would Boaz have pursued her if she had been another man's girlfriend? In all likelihood, probably not.

This is a biblical example of what can happen when you choose a healthy walk with Jesus by your side, and trust in his plan. That's what Ruth did. And her story turned into an incredible tale of redeeming love.

IT'S NEVER TOO LATE TO BEGIN HONORING GOD

Sometimes we need to stop hanging on to second best and let a relationship go. And sometimes, two people in a relationship *can* commit their lives and relationship to God and begin anew.

In other words, if you're currently in a relationship that is not honoring to God, it's important to dive in to scripture so that the truth of God can guide you to still waters and green pastures (Psalm 23:2). There is hope if you strengthen your relationship with God and do some hard inner work, then your relationship with each other may get a fresh start. We are not anyone's savior. Jesus is the ONLY one that can save someone. We have no power to do this. We are not God. Let God do his work and trust that his way is best. Isaiah 55:8-9 says "For my thoughts are not your thoughts, neither are your ways my ways," declares the Lord. "As the heavens are higher than the earth, so are my ways higher than your ways and my thoughts than your thoughts."

When I was a sophomore in college, I thought I was trying to pursue Jesus, but I was still quite lost. I lived in a sorority house, which allowed me to be influenced by my peers living in sin. Every weekend I would go out drinking and seek attention from boys. It was an endless, self-destructive cycle.

One night, I went to a fraternity party and met a young man. What happened next felt like a scene from a romantic movie. I was chatting with friends when a boy pulled me aside and struck up a conversation. For some reason, I brought up the topic of Jesus. (This was odd because while I believed in Jesus, I certainly wasn't following him in many areas of my life.)

Immediately, this guy said, "Stay here. I'll be right back."

When he returned, he handed me his cracked phone and said, "I would love to take you on a date away from this party scene if you'd let me. I would love your phone number if you feel comfortable giving it to me."

C'mon, girls. Can I get an amen?

Turns out, we were both Christians, but we were chasing the world instead of God. We went on a date and ended up having sex. For the next seven months, we completely idolized each other and did not put Christ in the center of our relationship.

Our actions cost us both a lot of pain.

When we broke up, we each acted out in hurtful and immature ways. Desperate for connection and affirmation, both of us reached out to fill the gap by using other people instead of taking the necessary time alone after a breakup. We decided to do stupid things with the first people who laid eyes on us. He slept with a girl, and I ended up leading a guy on. It was wrong and embarrassing and hurt both of us—and the people we used—deeply.

That summer, I attended an eight-week discipleship program through my campus ministry that changed my life. He spent the summer focusing on himself and God. At the end of the break, we got back together. This time, we had a renewed relationship with biblical expectations and healthy boundaries. Plus, we were committed to honoring God. What did this mean? For one, we stopped having sex. Not only that, but we stopped doing a lot of things that were impure. At times, we were imperfect and were tempted by our flesh. Throughout this time, we learned about God's forgiveness and grace. God also redeemed our relationship by showing us what it meant to follow him while dating. God showed his love through our imperfections and to feel fully known by the grace God gives.

God is the ultimate Redeemer. He transformed both of our lives, and he deepened our relationship with each other. Our decision to prioritize God encouraged other couples we knew to put God first, experience the love that God gives us, and establish sexual boundaries.

Wherever you are in life, a relationship with Jesus is exactly what you need—and then everything else will follow. It is never too late to repent and let God do it his way. He turns evil into good. He takes your messy story and transforms it into a redemptive reunion.

HONORING GOD DOESN'T KEEP US FROM PAIN

That guy and I dated for two years, which dramatically impacted my life. We eventually broke up because we were neglecting God's calling for our individual purposes. We had put so much time into our relationship that we stopped putting time and effort into continuing to work on ourselves. We were idolizing each other instead of making space for God to speak into our individual purposes and lives.

That was a little more than a year ago.

My heart is still burdened today. In fact, I feel an overwhelming sense of loneliness. Maybe it's because I often spend too much time scrolling through Instagram feeds of couples getting engaged or people posting about amazing jobs or vacations.

Maybe it's because I drove through my college town today and got flooded with good memories that belong to a closed chapter in my life. Well, some are good memories, and some are memories I wish I could forget. For nostalgia's sake, I drove past my ex-boyfriend's former house. I quickly realized this wasn't a healthy choice because it left me distracted, overwhelmed, sad, and flooded with memories of the times I spent there. So many bad and good memories in one location.

I think the hardest part of singleness for me is when I find myself focusing on worldly things and then go down a spiral of overthinking: the memories, the wishes, the fantasies, and the raw feelings.

I have to constantly remind myself *why* singleness is a good thing because it for sure doesn't feel *good* most of the time. There are times where I feel on top of the world and so content with where I am; then there are times I feel like I just ran as fast as I could into a brick wall, and my whole insides feel like they are dying.

Today has been one of those days. I feel burdened and sapped of life and vitality. I feel like that one episode of *The Office* when Michael sees Holly and A. J. together at the Christmas party and says, "I am dying inside."

Breakups suck. Especially when it takes a long time to get over someone.

If you are going through a breakup or trying to get over someone, take heart. Be kind to yourself. Be patient. It's okay to lean on Jesus through these moments and to not force yourself to move on. I have learned that it's important to cling to the truths and grace Jesus gives us instead of being in a state of mind of constant comparison and "what if's."

HONORING GOD GIVES US THE STRENGTH TO WAIT FOR GOD'S BEST

How many of you hate the phrase: "Singleness is a gift"? The number of times I have heard that from campus ministers and church leaders makes me cringe. However, 1 Corinthians 7 says otherwise.

So, what does it really mean to see singleness as a gift? How can I see singleness as a gift?

Develop your relationship with Jesus and dive deeper into discovering the root of the lies you are believing. I believed in the lie that I had to please my boyfriend, my parents and even Jesus. I came to find out the point of any relationship is to point and direct one another toward Jesus, and to delight in him and in God's creation.

I encourage you to read Scripture and recognize that the culture we live in may be feeding us lies. I often refer to Job 31 and Proverbs 31 to remind myself what a godly man and a godly woman look like. In the meantime, learn to love who God created you to be and seek to become the person Jesus called you to be.

Also, in my singleness, I've learned that—as I seek God—he gives me dreams, passions, and goals to pursue. In fact, I'm able to write this book because I am single and not distracted. I found out that singleness is a gift because we get to give full devoted attention to God alone. We can find complete intimacy in him. We don't need someone else to provide us with those desires.

There might be something God is calling you to do while you are single. Ask him. Listen for his answer.

Jesus is with us in every season of our lives. He is with us in our waiting, in our trusting, and in our working. He is the master gardener, the one working in our harvests.

John 15:1–4 says, "I am the true vine, and my Father is the gardener. He cuts off every branch in me that bears no fruit, while every branch that does bear fruit he prunes so that it will be even more fruitful. You are already clean because of the word I have spoken to you. Remain in me, as I also remain in you. No branch can bear fruit by itself; it must remain in the vine. Neither can you bear fruit unless you remain in me."

God has spoken to me in such a calming way about singleness. He gave me these words for encouragement: *trusting*, *working*, and *waiting*. Notice the "ing" on the ending because all of these are an action of what we need to be doing in our time of singleness.

Trusting comes in waves; it's not a one-and-done type of thing. It's an ongoing process of continuing to trust in Jesus when hardships and dry seasons happen. Trust takes work.

Working is a challenge, at best, but it's often downright hard too. Working on yourself is important during singleness. It requires actively moving toward Jesus with every decision even if it brings sacrifice. On the fourth of July not long ago, I was given an amazing opportunity to go boating in California with two of my best friends from college. It would have been a blast and a trip of a lifetime. However, as I started praying about it, conviction hit me. I knew that if I were to go on that trip, I would have fallen into the temptation of drunkenness, opening the possibility of spiraling into sin. As we are working on ourselves and why we are the way that we are, it allows us to see Jesus clearer. This is the process of sanctification. This comes with sacrifice, patience, and waiting.

Waiting is something we all must learn to endure, and along the way faith is often increased as we come to rely on Jesus as a result. We find ourselves waiting for a job to start, waiting to find roommates and leases, waiting to graduate, waiting for where God is calling us next. Confession: I'm impatient! I would rather cut in line than have to wait. When seasons change and things become new, it's painful for me. Waiting for what's next is painful. Waiting for marriage, waiting to get a job offer, waiting for healing, waiting for an answer. I don't like waiting. Honestly, who does? But I know that waiting builds character. It can bring healing. It can bring greater confidence through the discernment we experience. What we do in the waiting matters. Serving at a church, memorizing scripture, having godly mentors speak in our lives. These are all some examples of what I have done in the waiting.

For all you women reading this: What if you believed that you genuinely didn't need a man? That you didn't need a boyfriend to fill up those needs of yours. What if you truly believed that all you need is the love of Jesus? What if I told you that the more you work on loving yourself by receiving the love of Jesus and giving it all to him, you will be fulfilled and satisfied.

So put that phone down before you text that crush or that boy who takes forever to text you back. Instead, have some endurance to pursue your dreams and be who God called you to be. You are seen and you are loved by God—whether you feel that love or not.

Jesus is here to make you feel loved and doesn't want you to settle for someone that makes you feel stressed and insecure. He fulfills your deepest needs and desires. He is not finished with you yet. In fact, he is just beginning.

I dated a boy in high school who I expected to give me all the love I needed. But he couldn't possibly give that to me, and I regret not investing that time with godly girlfriends and mentors.

The point of a relationship and marriage is to put Jesus first and to love each other deeper because Jesus is working though you.

Remind yourself of these things by diving into Scripture and what it says and seeking counsel from people you trust.

This can help you understand how much Jesus loves you and also help you recognize and reject unrealistic expectations for the relationships that you have around you. A relationship with anyone is about the grace and forgiveness when we make mistakes. If we end up marrying someone, we're not marrying a list of perfect qualities; we marry an imperfect and broken person. Much like ourselves.

Ask God to prepare your heart now to be forgiving and loving to the people around you. Put your pride away and know that everyone has room for improvement and has areas in which they can still grow—including yourself and the person you may end up with. Surrounding yourself with people who treat you with the love of Jesus is critical if we want to grow to become more like Jesus.

I was always looking for the perfect guy. In fact, I focused so much on the list of what I wanted in a man that I forgot that there's not a man on earth who can meet all of my expectations. But while no guy is perfect like Jesus, there are guys out there who are forgiving and loving like Jesus because they have allowed him into their hearts.

Ask God to bring people into your life who love Jesus more than they love you. And if you love Jesus more than anyone else, that is a good starting point. It will keep you from idolizing someone or something and, instead, help you focus on how to glorify Jesus together.

HONORING GOD KEEPS US FOCUSED

I went through my journals from the end of high school and all throughout college. It came to my attention that the majority of those journals were filled with prayers and prayers regarding ex-boyfriends. It was honestly kind of overwhelming to realize that I had spent so many years distracted from God's purpose because of boys.

I thought about the girls I could have influenced and poured life into. I didn't maximize those relationships because I was so preoccupied with feelings and prayers for guys who weren't good for me at the time.

It made me realize that during seasons when I am single and not distracted, I can be the person others can call at 3:00 a.m. if they need a ride home from making a drunken mistake. I can bless others by having a house open twenty-four seven for girls to come and share their messes and their joys.

Being single brings me less distractions of this world. I have grown immensely closer to Jesus because I am not constantly thinking about how to "do more" or fix a broken relationship. Just because I am single doesn't mean that I don't have any distractions. Boys still distract me. Temptation still distracts me. The difference with me now is that I create boundaries for myself to protect my heart and thoughts from leading me astray. I found a deeper intimacy and truth in the Lord because I was able to fully recognize that I didn't need a man to satisfy my desires. All I need is Jesus.

JENNY'S STORY

There are three truths I had to remind myself of during my college years as my friends were getting engaged while I was still single and alone, craving a relationship: 1) marriage is a calling, and 2) singleness is a calling. Both are equally holy to God, and both are equally used by God to purify our hearts so that we may look more like him. That is the purpose of every calling and every season God walks through with us—to look more like Jesus.

This leads me to the last truth I highly valued because it took a lot of pressure off of me and anyone who seemed to be boyfriend potential. We are often shocked to discover this truth once the pressure to make a good first impression on a cute guy falls away and the walls of our hearts come down: 3) The person you are going to marry, God willing, is far from perfect, and so are you. In fact, Scripture says no one is good—not even one (Romans 3:10). And honestly, *praise God for that.*

If the man I married was perfect, what more could I offer him? I would contribute nothing to him. I would derive no purpose from our marriage. So, I praise God for the "thorn in my flesh" (2 Corinthians 12:7) and the thorn in his. Jesus states, "My grace is sufficient for you, for my power is made perfect in weakness" (2 Corinthians 12:9). I can delight in his weaknesses and in mine, for when we are weak, then we are made stronger *together.*

Have you ever wondered whether we would be able to access the same level of intimacy with Jesus if we weren't broken? Think about it. Our desperate dependency on Jesus is only necessary because of our brokenness. And this dependency results in an incomparable intimacy. While we are not to be dependent on our spouse like we are on Jesus, I believe the intimacy I share with my fiancé, Ben, would not be nearly as deep if it weren't for the many trials and struggles we've walked through together.

And that's why our expectations should never fall on our partner in the first place, assuming our partner is actively pursuing God. Instead, our expectations should fall on the Holy Spirit dwelling within him, who is leading and guiding his steps. If your partner loves Jesus, the fruit of the Spirit will naturally flow according to God's will, not yours.

Sometimes, the fruit of his flesh will also show, and that's okay. Yours does too. We still live in these broken bodies that get the best of us from time to time. But our sin never gets to have the final say on who we are after we have been made a new creation in Christ. You are chosen by God. That's the truest thing about any of us.

Why do I follow Jesus? Because the love he fills me with is the only thing I have to offer to Ben. I couldn't truly love Ben without knowing Jesus. Why? Because Jesus *is* love.

Learn more about the relationship of Ruth and Boaz and how their relationship honored God (Ruth 4).

——— REFLECTION QUESTIONS ———

1. How can you honor God whether you are single or in a relationship?

2. Why is it important to read, know, and follow the scriptures that instruct us about honoring God in our relationships?

3. Why should you not give up on wanting a God-centered marriage/relationship instead of a worldy one?

4. What is distracting you in your daily life from putting
    God first?

5. What honorable attributes do you hope to have in ten
    years (spiritually, personally, relationally) if you start
    today and change your negative thoughts into positive
    ones?

6. Why do you feel lonely, and what can bring you closer to
    Jesus during this time?

CHAPTER 3

FIGHTING THE
GOOD FIGHT

Why Persevere in Times of Hardship and Pain?

When I was in fourth grade, I was sitting in the library of my elementary school when I received a note telling me to go to the office because my mom was on the phone. As soon as I picked up the phone, my mom shared the devastating news: my grandma had just had a massive stroke and was in the hospital.

My heart broke at that moment, and I was devastated even though I had no idea what a "massive stroke" meant. All I knew was that my grandma was in pain and in the hospital.

Flash-forward one year.

My grandma moved into the basement of our home, which was remodeled to accommodate her disabilities after her stroke.

To answer your question: Yes, we have one of those stair lifts that you see in movies.

For six years, my grandma lived with us, being cared for by my loving and servant-hearted mom. My grandma's left side of her brain was affected from the stroke. This meant she couldn't move her right arm and had minimal access to her right leg. It also meant that her speech was impaired.

To this day, she still speaks gibberish. But even though she can't speak clearly, she is able to understand and comprehend her surroundings. My grandma grasps everything going on but can't translate her thoughts into coherent speech.

Can you imagine not being able to communicate verbally with others? How heartbreaking. Today, my grandma is in a nursing home, unable to voice thoughts, feelings, or memories. And yet, she still demonstrates joy and love with the people who surround her. This includes family, friends, and the staff at the nursing home.

Despite the damages of the stroke on her mind and body, she continues to show me how to experience and share the heart of Jesus. My grandma displays joy and love by listening, giving hugs, choosing to trust in Jesus, and showing a genuine interest in my life. She shares the gospel through the way she lives, not through words.

WHEN OTHERS ARE STRUGGLING, YOU CAN MAKE A DIFFERENCE

Sharing the truth of the gospel and what Jesus did on the cross is critical because that is what brings us freedom. But too many people have heard the gospel without any love. People are looking at American Christians rather than followers of Jesus, which is heartbreaking because most of these people are not displaying the love of Jesus. Let your actions mirror what you say and believe (1 John 3:18).

We need to use our gifts, our time, and our abilities to spread the word, to serve, to show people love, and (most importantly) to know God's love. Our gifts don't mean a thing if they are not at the feet of Jesus.

Yes, there will be pain, disappointment, and destruction in this world. But now is the time to fight. Fight for our faith. Fight for Jesus. Fight for others to be exposed to the true gospel. Fight for lives to be changed.

The American culture tells us to run and work hard. God tells us to rely on him and go at a slow pace (Isaiah 40:31).

There is no room for disrespectfully arguing or hatred at a time like this. It's okay to have disagreements with others, but many argue with out displaying any love or care for that person. Love people. This is the answer: LOVE. The gospel can get diminished because a lot of "Christians" aren't showing the love that Jesus did. They know what Jesus did for them but haven't fully grasped what that means for their life.

What if we lived how my grandma, sweet Joyce, lives? How much would we be able to change the movement of Christianity if we loved and genuinely took an interest in other peoples' lives? What if we saw our enemies, the homeless, and random people we meet as if they were Christ himself?

EVEN WHEN THE WORLD SUCKS, LOVE HELPS

Perhaps you're thinking, *How can I love others when others don't love me? How can I love others when the world is attacking me? How can I love others when there isn't justice for the horrific acts being displayed? How am I supposed to love others and fight this "good fight" when it doesn't feel good?*

You're right. This world is filled with racism. This world is filled with hate. This world is filled with so many endless, bad things. But Jesus isn't from this world. God sent Jesus to fix this world by allowing him to die on the cross. God wants to fix this world, even more than we do, that's why he created this rescue plan. Even if it doesn't look or feel like it at the moment, Jesus is coming back for us so that this world will be renewed like God intended for it to be. God feels our pain and deep sorrows. But even knowing this, sometimes, I don't understand why things happen the way they do. I don't have all the answers of why bad things happen in this world, but I do know that God is a good and loving Father.

Despite the terrible things around us, we can have the confidence to choose to love because Jesus loves us at our worst.

Jesus chose to love me when I was doing bad things. We have Jesus to help us love others who are doing bad things.

The song "Sparrow and Lilies" by Pat Barrett comes to mind with fighting the good fight. Some key lyrics that resonate with me are: "Hold on, Love, things are gonna get better. I know it's hard." Our hope isn't in this world. It's in Jesus.

It takes some fighting to get to this point. Fighting to gain the fruits of the spirit: love, joy, peace, forbearance, kindness, goodness, faithfulness, gentleness, and self-control (Galatians 5:22–23). It's a tough thing to do. In order to get to this point, we need to die to ourselves and let Jesus take the wheel in our life (que Carrie Underwood).

Remembering why we need to display these qualities is crucial. Loving the way Jesus loves can allow others to get a sense of heaven. I know that this can be difficult; you're talking to the queen of stubbornness, frustration, and anger! But even when these kinds of emotions threaten to overwhelm us, we can get through it by leaning on Jesus, Scripture, godly counsel, godly thoughts, and his strength. Matthew 11:28-30 says, "Come to me, all who are weary and burdened, and I will give you rest. Take my yoke upon you and learn from me, for I am gentle and humble in heart, and you will find rest for your souls. For my yoke is easy and my burden is light."

Loving the way Jesus loves can allow others to get a sense of heaven.

It is okay to let those angry emotions out in a godly manner. I found boxing as a relief to take my frustrations out physically. This may look like going on a run, screaming in your car, or physically hitting something—like boxing or hitting a baseball with a bat!

It is also important to know where the root of these emotions are coming from and to work through them with the truth of God and perhaps even talking with a friend or counselor. It's okay to tell God that you are angry with him. I tell my parents that I am mad at them, so God doesn't expect us to only bring him our smiles.

EVEN WHEN GOD DOESN'T FIX YOUR CIRCUMSTANCES, YOU CAN STILL TRUST HIM WITH YOUR HEART

I was listening to a young adults podcast the other day, and something the pastor said stuck with me: "God cares more about our hearts than our circumstances." How many times have you been stuck in a situation that has brought you pain and anxiety? How often have you wanted your circumstances to change so you can move on to another season?

I have been in this position more times than I can count. When my parents were filing for divorce, I prayed for God to intervene and change my circumstances. He didn't. In fact, there are many painful circumstances that he doesn't immediately eliminate: rejection, death, heartbreak, and abuse. You name it!

We've all experienced these types of human devastations. These experiences aren't from God; they are created by sin in this world. But God sees the big picture. He sees how painful things will help us grow. He grieves and he hurts with us, but he also sees the outcome. Revelation 21:4 says "He will wipe every tear from their eyes. There will be no death or mourning or crying or pain, for the old order of things has passed away." One day we will no longer be living in suffering.

When my parents were going through their divorce, it was painful for me. Being surrounded by constant fighting and having to be the mediator between them left me feeling angry, frustrated, and in extreme emotional pain. But those circumstances eventually made me stronger and helped shaped me into the person I am today.

God didn't answer my prayers the way I wanted him to, but he cared about my heart more than he did the circumstances. He wanted me to have joy, and share my story of redemption. God is faithful, and he redeems our pain and our hearts even when he doesn't always redeem our circumstances.

Look at John 4, for example. The Samaritan woman was sleeping around with men who weren't satisfying her heart and only bringing her pain. I guarantee you that she was praying to God and pleading with him to get out of her messy situation. Then Jesus came along; he was waiting for her at the well. Waiting for her to come to him when it was hot and uncomfortable.

The Samaritan woman had a life-changing interaction with Jesus that empowered her to drop everything and run to the townspeople who had shunned her to tell them about Jesus. This woman went from someone who was rejected and shunned to someone who brought the life-changing news of Jesus to the whole town.

When there is

- pain that is unbearable,
- grief that won't go away,
- circumstances you think will never end, and
- prayers you're not sure God even hears,

I urge you to fight that good fight toward Jesus. *Why?* Because the other side is filled with joy, redemption, and faithfulness. God always fulfills his promises.

WHEN WE ARE IN TROUBLE OR IN PAIN, WE GET TO EXPERIENCE GOD

When I was in fourth grade, I had really bad OCD (obsessive compulsive disorder). I had to tap light switches about forty times, in a particular way, before I left a room. If I didn't fulfill this compulsion, I felt like I was going to die. I would have to blink a certain way, or I felt like I was going to die. These thoughts and compulsive actions all developed after my uncle had a tragic death by overdosing on drugs and alcohol. I had a fear of death and a fear that if I did one thing wrong, my family or I would die too.

After praying for my OCD to go away throughout high school and fully being obedient to Jesus, I was redeemed and saved from OCD and haven't struggled with it since. *How good is our God? God is the one that brings us hope and miracles.*

One morning, I learned another valuable lesson about asking for help. I woke up, chugged a whole pot of cold-brew coffee, and decided to do the mini-incline in Castle Rock, Colorado. For those of you who have no clue what that is, it's basically a set of two hundred stairs that goes up a hill.

I thought that coffee would bring me energy and a small granola bar would provide the necessary strength to go up and down this thing a couple of times. I was wrong, and I was humbled.

I went running up these stairs at full speed with pride rising because I kept passing people. Within ten seconds, my breath practically went out on me, and I didn't think I could get up the last fifty steps. I finally got to the top and became extremely dizzy and nauseous. I had to lay down on the bench at the top. Weakness overpowered me, and I prayed that God would give me strength because I physically couldn't get up without feeling like I was going to pass out.

This was a moment I felt much like Michael Scott in the episode of *The Office* where he ate a bunch of chicken alfredo for the 5K and ended up in the hospital because he was dehydrated.

Michael had so much pride built up that he thought he could prepare right before the race and then ended up getting humbled real fast. I wonder how many of us do that. We think we can do something on our own, then we end up getting humbled and feel like we don't have control of our lives anymore.

Here's the thing about this incline. I only needed two things to make me feel better: 1) water, 2) and someone to help pick me back up.

How much would your life shift if you humbled yourself and drank the living water Jesus is offering you? Boom roasted (another of many references from *The Office* for the die-hard fans). This verse encourages me: "If you knew the gift of God and who it is that asks you for a drink, you would have asked him and he would have given you **living water**" (John 4:10, emphasis added). We need to know the true character of God to understand why it is important to ask for living water.

I finally got back down the hill by descending the longer, shaded path. Humbling myself allowed God to lift me back up and get me down the mountain with provision and water (John 4:23).

But he didn't do it magically without any effort on my part. Like the crippled man Jesus healed in John 5:8, I needed to get up and walk.

Hebrews 10:36 reminds us why we persevere, "You need to persevere so that when you have done the will of God, you will receive what he has promised."

MERCY'S STORY

One of my first memories growing up is being homeless. Empty pantries and refrigerators were a staple of my childhood. Maybe your family lived comfortably financially, but then your parents' marriage ended in divorce. Maybe you were abused. Maybe you lost a family member or friend. Maybe you or someone in your home was chronically ill, and you grew up watching them suffer.

If you are like me, the American gospel told you it would all be okay. Throughout this experience, I attended church and prayed faithfully. I believed if I were good enough, things would finally work out. If I served in enough ministries, maybe my mom would be healed. If I never doubted God's goodness for a second, maybe God would reward my pain with a platform. Maybe I'd get comfort instead of a cross.

Maybe you labored for years under this false hope. Maybe you served yourself into exhaustion, prayed your throat sore, and smiled until your cheeks hurt, but your loved one still died. The abuse did not stop. The pain did not go away. You did not understand.

Maybe there has been a time in your life when you wondered, *What is the purpose of pain?*

In the book of Job, a blameless man suffers the loss of his livelihood, his health, and his children. His wife advises him to abandon his faith, and his closest friends shame him. After several chapters listening to this horrible advice, God breaks onto the scene with an impassioned defense of his own goodness and power.

How does Job respond? He looks to heaven and says, "I had only heard about you before, but now I have seen you with my own eyes."

Do we want to see God, or do we just want to hear about him? Christ's transforming love is most revealed not in a life of ease, but in a life of homelessness, persecution, and betrayal, followed by a violent death. The goodness of God is most vividly displayed not in comfort, but in a cross.

We persevere because Christ persevered for us. We endure so we can learn to be joyful in hope, patient in affliction, and faithful in prayer (Romans 12:12). We love (and keep loving) others because God loves us. We have hope because whether or not God fixes our circumstances, he heals our hearts.

We don't give up because we want to see God.

Learn more about Job preserving in his faith. He was in extreme pain and sorrow. Yet through this, Job stayed true to God and his faith (Job 1-31).

──────── REFLECTION QUESTIONS ────────

1. Why do you continue to follow Jesus when you can't see the results?

2. Why does the Bible tell us to preserve and fight the good fight?

3. Why do I still follow Jesus when bad things happen?

4. Why do I believe God is good when the world he created is so bad and full of sin? How can I believe he is good?

CHAPTER 4

CHOOSE JOY

Why Should We Pray and Never Give Up?

I was sitting in my dorm room on my lofted bed, feeling dark and empty. I picked up my first prayer journal, grabbed a pen, and wrote down my prayers. I prayed for godly friends to surround me. I talked to God about how I was desperate to gain healthy friendships.

One year later, my prayers were answered. God surrounded me with an amazing group of Christian women who still stand by my side today. God wants to answer your prayers, so that you can have a deeper faith in him.

But it doesn't always feel that way, does it? Perhaps your frustrations sounds something like this:

> "I have prayed for the last ten years that they would come to Christ, and they are farther away than ever before."

"I have constantly prayed to be financially stable, and
I am still in debt."

"I've prayed for healing, and I'm still sick."

"I've prayed for companionship, and I'm still alone."

These soul-crushing experiences can lead us to ask a heart-felt question: "Why continue to pray when it feels like God isn't even here?"

I hear you. I don't know what it's like to be in your shoes, and I have no room to tell you what to do. But consider this:

What if God's timing and plan is different than ours?

What if God is planning on answering that prayer in the future?

What if God has a hold on our lives better than we think or can see?

What if God wants us to look at our circumstances in another perspective?

PRAYER AND PERSISTENCE CHANGES LIVES

I want to tell you about a dark crisis my family went through, including an experience I had with prayer that moves me to this day.

When I was a junior in high school, my dad invited a young man named Bennett, the son of one of his friends, to stay with him and help get him back on his feet. Bennett was a mentor to my brother, and they bonded over sports and other boy stuff. They developed a deep friendship throughout the three years that Bennett lived at my dad's house.

On February 15, 2018, my dad was coming home from a long day of work and picked up my brother from school. For the last couple of hours, my dad had been concerned that Bennett was not answering any of his phone calls or text messages.

As my dad pulled into the driveway, he had a strange feeling that something was not right. When he walked into the house and spotted my dog through the outside window in the freezing cold waiting to get let in, that feeling intensified. My dad sprinted up the stairs in complete panic mode while my brother stayed downstairs. Running into Bennett's room, my dad found Bennett pale, unconscious, and laying in the middle of the floor.

My dad frantically performed CPR on Bennett and then grabbed his phone and dialed 911. The next five minutes felt like hours. As the loud sirens started to come down the street and pull into my driveway, my dad led the paramedics upstairs in a panic. Bennett had relapsed, overdosed, and passed away.

I got the call from my sister telling me Bennett had overdosed.

My heart broke, and my body went numb.

I couldn't stand up and went in complete panic mode. Three girls came and rushed by my side as they heard my cry.

They held my hand and prayed over me for the next thirty minutes.

I couldn't stop thinking about the pain my dad and my brother were going through in that moment. My brother, in particular, was reeling from the pain. Someone close to him had died a tragic death, and he couldn't make sense of what had happened.

My brother became furious with God and with the world. I had shared the gospel with him and the truth about Jesus too many times to count. But he was not ready to make the decision to follow Jesus. It felt as if nothing anyone said to him about God was sinking in. He fought against everything.

So, I prayed.

I prayed over my brother, pleading that he would forgive God. That he would come to fully accept Jesus in his heart and trust him. I prayed that my brother would get connected in a youth group and even be in a leadership position within the church someday. I prayed that God would fulfill his purpose in life and use my brother for the sake of God's will. I prayed for my brother's story to impact others. I even prayed that my brother would desire to become a pastor or play some role in ministry in the future. I prayed that he was able to receive the love of Christ.

I prayed that his *pain* would bring *joy*.

Five months later, I got a phone call from my brother that brought me to tears. He called to tell me he had accepted Christ in his heart and that, from this day forward, he would pursue Jesus. He got baptized that same day at the Christian camp he was attending. I have never felt that much joy in my life.

I wept. My prayers for my brother had been answered. But here's the really crazy part: while I prayed *detailed* prayers, those *detailed* prayers had gotten answered.

My brother didn't just get involved in a youth group; he ended up being on the high school leadership team. On top of that, a mentor came into his life whom he would meet with weekly. He now has a godly relationship with a girl that loves Jesus and feels the calling in his heart to be in vocational ministry someday.

I am shaken.

Praise God. God completely surprised me. And it all started with one prayer.

God brings awful and traumatic experiences into a redemption story. He brings death to life. Even though it may seem impossible at the time:

- God is faithful. (Psalm 33:4)
- God is a Redeemer. (Psalm 19:14)
- God is present. (Psalm 139:7-12)

WHEN WE PRAY, GOD DWELLS

God didn't stop there. My brother had the opportunity to share his testimony multiple times on stage, speaking to thousands of high schoolers. This tragic experience became a part of his testimony that impacted other people. But even if my brother had just accepted Jesus, that would have been enough. He didn't need to be doing anything else on top of that.

The parable of the prodigal son tells the story of a son who ran away from home, spent all of his money, and was left empty and broken. When the son returned home, his father welcomed him with open arms and threw a party for him. Likewise, we don't need to work to earn God's love. He loves us right where we are. **He loves us when we don't love him.** That's the point of the gospel. He loves us so much; he wants to save us and live with us for eternity.

We don't need to work to earn God's love. He loves us right where we are.

This is *why* I pray.

This is *why* I don't stop praying.

This is *why* praying is important. You can change someone's life, even your life, in prayer. You get to be a part of God's will and see the impact your small or big prayers have amidst your family and across the world. You get to know the love of God and build a relationship with him. You get to talk to the God of the universe (Ephesians 2:18). Through Jesus, we have access to a relationship with our loving God. How amazing is that?

Sometimes prayers aren't answered in the way you want, though, or they are not answered quickly. Don't give up, my friend. Push through and continue to talk and sit with God.

It is hard to continue when you don't see any results, but I can promise you that God has a hand on your situation. He has a plan even if it feels like the world is falling apart.

Here's what I have learned about prayer:

- God sits with us in our hurt. He cries with us. He feels our pain (Psalm 34:18).
- God knows our prayers even when we don't say anything (Psalm 139:4).
- God cares deeply about our desires (Psalm 37:4).
- God wants us to talk to him about our day and how we are feeling (Psalm 23).
- God is waiting for you to talk to him today: in your car, through your journal writings, while taking a walk (John 15:7).

When you talk to God, he dwells: "Lord, I love the house where you live, the place where your glory dwells" (Psalm 26:8).

JACQUELINE'S STORY

I grew up thinking that life was about winning. I gave my life to it, but it was subtle. I wanted to be the best at everything because it seemed to create results that made me feel like I was enough. This looked like being a part of every sports team, getting straight A's, and being in the so-called "popular group." I still went to church on the weekends, but I was living for myself. I was only concerned with what I wanted and with what made me happy.

I got enough "Jesus" to feel like a good person, and then I'd continue on with my life. But I always felt like I was missing out on something. I was pretty content doing life on my own terms a little longer. It wasn't until college when I realized this wasn't enough.

I moved to Colorado where I immersed myself deep into the party scene, sorority life, a codependent relationship, and high-achievement mode all at the same time. From the world's standards, I had it all. And yet, it wasn't enough. I still felt unsatisfied.

At the time, I was going to my sorority's Bible study and felt God calling me in deeper, but I had no idea what it meant. It was terrifying and exciting. I decided to give my life to God and make him Lord of my life. I experienced peace and joy unlike before. I was also dating a boy I cared about, but I felt like God wanted me to find myself apart from him. Though this boy meant a lot to me, I wanted him to find Jesus too.

I prayed for God to use this relationship for his glory and to soften his heart to love Jesus as much as I was starting to. After a few months of prayer and talking about Jesus, his atheist mindset became open and interested. Then shortly after, unexpectedly and tragically, his younger brother passed away.

I had no idea how he was going to respond to this and what God was doing in it either. But I kept praying. I prayed this guy wouldn't hate God for his brother's death but would somehow run toward him. In the midst of excruciating pain and overwhelming sorrow, he was convinced God was real and eventually decided to follow Jesus.

I saw how God's redemptive grace can overwhelm the most horrific situations, how powerful prayer was, and how good God truly is. After experiencing this, I trusted in Jesus even more and knew my life would never be the same. I will never forget how God answered those tear-filled prayers in the most incredible way. Ultimately, God led us in different directions, but we both made our way back to Jesus. I quickly realized that life isn't about winning. I now wanted my life to be about loving a good God and praying that others would come to love him too.

Learn more about Hannah's story in scripture and how God had answered her prayers when she wasn't seeing results. 1 Samuel 1:1-2, 6, 9-11, 19-20

——— REFLECTION QUESTIONS ———

1. Why do I pray?

2. Why do I avoid praying?

3. Why is praying something we must continue to do on a daily basis?

4. What does the Bible say about praying?

5. Do I believe my prayers will be answered? Why or why not?

6. Describe a time where God has answered you or someone you know prayers.

CHAPTER 5

THE BIGGER PICTURE

Why Should We Delight in the Lord and in His Purpose for Our Lives?

I love the outdoors. I find so much joy and peace when I am sitting outside. Whether it's in the mountains, by a lake, or on a beach, I seem to feel the nearness of God in those places. Because I love the outdoors so deeply, spontaneous trips speak close to my heart.

On one such trip, I discovered the perfect camping spot right next to a calming river. Surrounded by beauty, I was laying in my hammock, listening to the sound of rushing water and talking to God. In the process, I reflected on how much I have grown this past year and about how my journey throughout college brought me to where I am at today.

I discovered my true self this past year and chose to trust God in my purpose and who he has created me to be. Thinking about this allowed me to *delight* in God. Delighting in God brings me an indescribable feeling of peace:

- Peace that God is working in my life
- Peace that shows God cares more about my life than I ever could
- Peace that takes my worries about the future away

I delighted in God and let God delight in me by reading Psalm 139 in my hammock. Can we just take a moment to let Psalm 139 sink in?

> You have searched me, Lord,
> and you know me.
> You know when I sit and when I rise;
> you perceive my thoughts from afar.
> You discern my going out and my lying down;
> you are familiar with all my ways.
> Before a word is on my tongue
> you, Lord, know it completely.
> You hem me in behind and before,
> and you lay your hand upon me.
> Such knowledge is too wonderful for me,
> too lofty for me to attain.
>
> Where can I go from your Spirit?
> Where can I flee from your presence?

If I go up to the heavens, you are there;
if I make my bed in the depths, you are there.
If I rise on the wings of the dawn,
if I settle on the far side of the sea,
even there your hand will guide me,
your right hand will hold me fast.
If I say, "Surely the darkness will hide me
and the light become night around me,"
even the darkness will not be dark to you;
the night will shine like the day,
for darkness is as light to you.

For you created my inmost being;
you knit me together in my mother's womb.
I praise you because I am fearfully and wonderfully made;
your works are wonderful,
I know that full well.
My frame was not hidden from you
when I was made in the secret place,
when I was woven together in the depths of the earth.
Your eyes saw my unformed body;
all the days ordained for me were written in your book
before one of them came to be.
How precious to me are your thoughts, God!
How vast is the sum of them!
Were I to count them,

they would outnumber the grains of sand—
when I awake, I am still with you.

If only you, God, would slay the wicked!
Away from me, you who are bloodthirsty!
They speak of you with evil intent;
your adversaries misuse your name.
Do I not hate those who hate you, LORD,
and abhor those who are in rebellion against you?
I have nothing but hatred for them;
I count them my enemies.
Search me, God, and know my heart;
test me and know my anxious thoughts.
See if there is any offensive way in me,
and lead me in the way everlasting.

The Lord knows what we love, and he knows our hearts better than we do.

The Lord *knows* us. He knows our *inmost being*. Isn't that incredible? God knew us while we were still in our mothers' wombs and planned good things for us *before* we even stepped foot on this earth. We were written in his book! I still can't wrap my head around that. The Lord *knows* what we love, and he knows our hearts better than we do.

GOD HAS EQUIPPED YOU TO FIND AND FULFILL YOUR PURPOSE

We are talking about two words. *I'll say them.*

The. Enneagram.

The Enneagram is often the topic of heated debate. You either hate it or are obsessed.

If you're not familiar with the Enneagram, it is a personality test that allows you to understand *why* you think and act the way you do. There are nine personalities identified by the test:

1. The Perfectionist

2. The Helper

3. The Achiever/Performer

4. The Romantic/Individualist

5. The Investigator

6. The Loyalist

7. The Enthusiast

8. The Challenger

9. The Peacemaker

I recommend taking the Enneagram test and looking in the back of this book for resources to learn more about your personality type. I also recommend you read the book *The Road*

Back to You by Ian Cron and Suzanne Stabile. I am (most likely) a 9 wing 8. This correlates to the Peacemaker with a wing of a Challenger.

My "personality type" is interesting because both of my characteristics contradict each other. For example, I will be going about my day, trying to avoid conflict (*Peacemaker*), then, all of a sudden, I want to challenge everything around me (*Challenger*).

I have a love/hate relationship with the enneagram.

The good news is that this personality test allowed me to learn about my area of weaknesses and strengths. For the first time in my life, I was able to fully name *why* I was acting and feeling a certain way. The bad news is that it also made me feel controlled or boxed in.

Don't let the Enneagram or another personality test put you in a box or allow you to only date certain people because you guys are the "most compatible" based on a test's interpretation of your personality type.

Don't let the Enneagram control your life. Let the Bible direct your life.

Don't let the Enneagram give you an excuse of your sin struggles. Repent and turn toward God daily.

Don't let the Enneagram "validate" how you treated someone or did something you shouldn't have done. Let God speak to you on your purpose. Follow the voice of God, not the voice of the creator of the Enneagram.

That said, the Enneagram and other personality tests can be amazing tools as you seek to understand more about who you are, why you are the way that you are, and what you're passionate about. They can help you find your *purpose*. But it's effective only when you use it in the context of Scripture and God's calling on your life.

PURSUING GOD'S PURPOSE FOR US FULFILLS OUR PASSIONS AND DREAMS

When I feel the most connected to myself, I feel closer to God. God wants us to simply be *us*. God delights in us just as we delight in him (but more so). When we enjoy the things we love, it glorifies God, as long as it aligns with the truth in the Bible.

I encourage you to lean into your dreams and passions.

Start with praying these words: "God, lead me, and reveal to me my passions, the desires of my heart, and your direction."

At a Christian camp, I prayed that simple prayer. I was a junior in high school and was freaking out. I was about to apply for colleges and had no clue where God wanted me to go. I had no idea what God's purpose for me might be.

During a worship night at this camp, I remember closing my eyes and listening to the music. I prayed, "Lord, I am freaking out and don't know what to do with my life. Please reveal to me and guide me where I need to be going."

I felt God whispering to me then. I thought his words were my own thoughts at first, but in the end I knew it was God directing me.

I began to dream about pursuing video for the purpose of documenting people's testimonies around the world. I have yet to fulfill that dream, but God's whisper led me into the field of journalism and media communications at Colorado State University.

I didn't think I would be writing a book in the meantime, but here I am.

I have learned over the last couple of years to not worry about my future because God has led me to the right spot by winging it and trusting him.

When I was in eighth grade, I was in a writing class that was geared to help the students get better in writing, spelling, and grammar. In other words, the kids who were below average in English would have to take this class. I hated this class because it made me feel like I was a failure and that I was looked down upon.

But now, I am an author.

My weakness in writing and my redemption story reminded me of Michael Jordan's story too. He was cut from the high school basketball team and then became a basketball legend. God has a purpose for our weaknesses.

One of my favorite verses is 2 Corinthians 12:9. "But he said to me, 'My grace is sufficient for you, for my power is made perfect in weakness.' Therefore, I will boast all the more gladly about my weaknesses, so that Christ's power may rest on me."

Your weaknesses will turn into your strengths when you lean on God's power. Look at Moses, for example. He had a stutter, but God used him to speak the word of God and deliver the Israelites into the promised land.

WE ARE NEVER ABANDONED—EVEN ON UNEXPECTED PATHS

COVID-19 ruined my plans for my college graduation and my future job. I had an entirely different plan than what God had in mind. Shortly after my virtual graduation, my dad and I planned a week-long road trip to Glacier National Park in Montana. However, this trip ended up not being the one we planned. It brought a whole bunch of ups and downs and ended up being a memory that will last forever.

The plan was to drive through Wyoming, continue on through Yellowstone National Park, and end up in Glacier National Park, then be on our way home. But when do our plans match up with what actually happens?

As my dad and I were planning our trip, we stumbled across an ad to rent a (discounted) Volkswagen bus. Obviously, we had to rent it. At the beginning of our road trip, my dad was in the driver's seat, driving the old, rustic Volkswagen bus. We had no air-conditioning, and the sound of the whistling fifty-mile-per-hour Wyoming wind rang in our ears. I had to hold my twenty-pound Lab in the back seat so she wouldn't slide around like crazy.

On top of that, the "check engine" light was on, and the beep from the warning continued to get louder and louder. We listened to this beep for the first day of our trip and ignored it. We ignored it to the point that we got stranded at a gas station because our van wouldn't start.

How often do we do this in our lives? How often do we ignore red flags and warnings from God, then we find ourselves broken and have nowhere else to turn?

I wonder what would have changed if we listened to these warning signs before they happened. However, God brings our negative stories into positive, life-changing messages regardless. Thank the Lord for that.

We weren't even a full two days into our trip and about an hour away from our next destination, Yellowstone National Park, and this VW bus shut down and wouldn't start on us. We became stranded at the gas station.

Although we looked like we had everything together and were the coolest people on the outside, we were struggling with the van's engine and our sanity on the inside. We had to get towed to a random, sketchy automobile repair shop in the middle of Cody, Wyoming.

When we got there, it looked like we just walked into a scene of the movie *Split*. No way out. Plus, one guy waiting for his RV literally looked exactly like the main character, James

McAvoy. It was terrifying because there was no way for us to get anywhere without this bus.

After a half day went by, I decided to put my pride and my "perfect image" down and text my small group, asking for prayers for our bus to get fixed. Prayers for my dad and I to get home safely, and to finish our trip as a bonus! Within the next minute, one girl from my small group messaged back and said her best friend lived in Cody, Wyoming. She could pick us up and bring us wherever we needed to go to get to a safer place.

Shortly after that, my dad got a text from the company who rented us the VW bus and they said they had two people on their way to pick the bus up and bring us a 2019 ProMaster camper van. On top of that, they booked us a hotel for no charge that allowed our dog to stay too. And that night there was a rodeo going on, so we weren't stuck in the middle of nowhere doing nothing. We had an amazing and memorable night in a small town at a rodeo.

This got me thinking.

Isn't this exactly how God is?

He uses a situation involving a beat-up, broken, damaged VW bus, and brings us into an air-conditioned, useful, purposeful, successful 2019 ProMaster camper van. He transformed something that wasn't getting anywhere into something that could get up mountains and see views. Plus, he provided us with help on that journey. We don't deserve it, *yet* God cares and loves us so much that he gives us so much more than we could ever fathom. Without God, this can't happen.

KNOWING GOD HAS A PLAN MEANS EVEN DISAPPOINTMENTS HAVE A PURPOSE

As I was entering our next campsite after a lack of service in Glacier National Park, I proceed to get a missed call and voicemail from my soon-to-be ministry internship in Estes Park, Colorado.

My heart sank as I knew that these missed calls probably meant bad news because he told me to call him back right away. I came to find out that the ministry internship was cancelled because of COVID-19.

But *why wasn't I as disappointed* as I thought I was going to be?

In fact, I felt the overwhelming presence of the Holy Spirit.

I knew this was in God's plan. He had already aligned my heart to prepare for that moment. God works in amazing ways. After this call, my best friend texted me within ten minutes, telling me that she got accepted into nursing school. It brought me so much joy, and the next hour was filled with so much comfort and community as we got to share our hope and excitement for the future and where God was going to lead us.

How cool is that?

On top of that, after finding out my fall plans had been cancelled, I received three more texts:

- I received a text from someone at church telling me they need my help in the video department in Fort Collins.

- I received a text from a friend telling me she had an open room in her place in Fort Collins. She needed someone to live with, and it was exactly within my budget.

- I received a follow-up text from my mentor, encouraging me to go through a spiritual growth program that worked perfectly for my schedule in Fort Collins.

God was clearly guiding and aligning my life to be in Fort Collins because everything was being shifted and handed to me, but not by my actions. I didn't need to *search for anything*, God *handed it to me*.

Sometimes finding God's purpose takes time and patience.

Sometimes God brings you things in order to build your character, patience, and fruits of the spirit rather than getting the result that you were hoping and praying for.

After making the decision to move to Fort Collins and signing a lease, I had to find a job. I didn't give God my full trust in this and instead poured my energy into trying to find one myself. I became frustrated that I started to lose hope and therefore became more impatient from rejection. But in the matter of a couple hours from my overthinking, God reminded me that he wanted me to be patient.

A sermon popped up on my YouTube feed where he spoke about patience. This sermon brought up the points about how sometimes it's not going to take more hard work to get something; instead, it's going to take waiting and patience while trusting God will provide.

May I point out something significant? Even if you don't fully agree with a pastor or a person's theology on everything, God can speak truth to you by the living Word of God and your personal convictions—as long as Jesus is in the center.

I thought I could find a job on my own, but I was quickly reminded that God is working when I am not. A job would come in his timing.

I moved to Fort Collins without a job, which was an unwise decision on the outside; inwardly, though, I knew that God was telling me to trust him and take a step of faith. I became overwhelmed in this process. I had to settle for a job that paid minimum wage in order to pay for rent. Before I got a check in the mail, I called my mom, bawling because I couldn't pay the extra $100 in rent and $25 in utilities.

I became humbled fast while working at my minimum-wage job. I looked around to see that there were a lot of other people struggling. Down-to-earth single moms, the wisest high-school and college dropouts, and lost people needing to find Jesus. It gave me the opportunity to praise Jesus for what I had and to pray and learn from the people whom I worked with.

Sometimes our plans are interrupted by God working on our character instead.

Two weeks later after working at this minimum-wage job, I got an email from an amazing company telling me that they wanted to interview me for a position they were creating from scratch. I didn't have to force my way into this job; they reached out to me.

In the second interview, they basically promised me this job. A week later, they offered me a job as a marketing coordinator and administrative assistant. God had this job planned out from the beginning. I just needed to trust that he would keep his promises.

God is so good. I was reminded that when I try and force things, they never work out. But if I simply pause and trust God, he will start handing and directing me to places I never thought were possible. This doesn't mean a pain-free life. It means a life with God walking next to me.

A year later, another dream job landed in my lap. It was a company that sends missionaries overseas to spread the good news of Jesus. It was a job that I prayed earnestly for, and God exceeded my dreams beyond what I could imagine. However, I felt as if God was teaching me that this job may be an open door in the *future* and not one for the season that I was in.

God taught me through that interview process that I didn't need to be a missionary to be loved by him. He loves me while working at a country club among rich people. I wasn't selfish not taking that job. God showed me that he loves me more than I could ever think or imagine. I can rest in the security of his love and by sharing his love with others, no matter where I am at.

ERIN'S STORY

"Is God even real? Is this all a lie? What if I am giving my life to something that is meaningless?"

These are the questions that were keeping me up at night as I tossed and turned in my bed. It started after I interviewed to work for my campus ministry. I left with a feeling of extreme vision, dreaming about souls on my campus being won for Christ. I was excited to see God work. I felt thankful for the work God had done in my life and was in awe of what I knew he would do next.

Then, out of nowhere, fear consumed me. I'm talking extreme anxiety. Doubt that felt disabling. I started asking myself questions that hadn't crossed my mind since I surrendered my life to Jesus at the beginning of college. As I lay in bed that night, I felt like my faith was eroding. I didn't know what to do. I knew God was real. I had put my faith in him and seen him radically change my life and the lives of others. So why was I doubting? And since I was, was my faith ever even real?

This season was dark and painful for me, and I felt alone. I didn't want to go to God because I felt like he was mad at me in my questioning of him. I didn't even know if he was there, let alone that I could ever be used for his glory.

In Matthew 28:17, Jesus appears to his disciples after his resurrection. Scripture says, "When they saw him, they worshipped him; but some doubted." Jesus' disciples, who experienced him more closely than anyone else, had a moment of doubt in their Savior. I began to realize I was not alone in my doubt. It was possible to simultaneously worship and doubt.

This was of great comfort to me. My doubt did not mean my faith was dead. In the text, immediately after, Jesus gives them the Great Commission: "Therefore go and make disciples of all nations, baptizing them in the name of the Father and of the Son and of the Holy Spirit, and teaching them to obey everything I have commanded you. And surely I am with you always, to the very end of the age" (Matthew 28:19–20).

In a moment where some of his closest followers experienced a moment of doubt, Jesus calls them deeper into obedience to him and promises his presence. He reminds them of his authority and his calling on their life. He promises he is with them always—not just in moments of great faith, but also in moments of doubt and weakness. I realized this calling and promise was true for me too.

God hadn't given up on me in my moments of doubt. He still wanted to use me for his kingdom. I began to view my doubt as a way that Jesus was refining me and pulling me closer to him through deeper steps of faith and obedience to his calling on my life, even when it was difficult (and it was). I follow Jesus because he promises me his presence through all seasons.

When I began to take my doubt directly to Jesus and continued to step further into obedience, even when I didn't see the point, he met me there. Through this, I have seen him use my doubt to strengthen my faith. I have learned a deeper dependence on him and a deeper understanding of my call to walking in obedience to Christ—even when it's hard. Why do I follow Jesus? Because he has given me purpose and meets me where I am through all seasons of life, including my doubt and brokenness.

Learn more about the way Jesus brings others a purpose throughout each of his encounters with ordinary people. John 4, Luke 5:17-29, John 17: 6-19, Matthew 7:7, Psalm 57:2, Ephesians 1:8-10

───── REFLECTION QUESTIONS ─────

1. How is God's purpose for your life working out for the greater good?

2. Why is it important for you to continue to follow God's purpose?

3. What do you love? Whom do you love?

4. What things make you genuinely happy?

5. Where do you feel closest to God?

6. Where do you feel most like yourself?

7. What do you do when you doubt God? What does the Bible say you should do?

CHAPTER 6

LOOKING IN THE MIRROR

Why Is It Important to Love Yourself?

I am twenty-three years old, and I have finally found the joy in being *Lindsea*. If you would have told me a year ago that I would finally find myself and learn to love me for me, I would have laughed and not believed you.

Looking back to the beginning of college and high school, I felt insecure and desired to be someone else. I was beyond scared to death that I was going to be judged: judged for who I am, rejected for who I am, and unloved.

I wanted to fit in. I choose not to speak and came off as brutally shy. I tried to find my identity in boys, popular girls, drinking, smoking, beauty, sex, cussing—you name it. I wanted to do what the cool kids were doing.

Deep down, I knew the things I was getting myself into didn't define me. But I let all these things drag me down. I was empty, connected to the wrong group of friends, and in a very dark place. I had lost hope—until I made it my priority to love Jesus. How did I do that? By letting God do the work and obeying him.

It is important to remember that God IS love and how much he loves you. We all make mistakes; I have made my fair share. "You are your biggest critic" was the most appropriate saying to describe my feelings toward myself in those years. Throughout my life, I have struggled with body image. I have always seen myself heavier than I am while feeling the impossible pressure of looking like the skinny girls everyone had crushes on in high school.

But here I am, same body shape and weight, for the most part, and I have accepted and loved myself for all my "perceived" flaws. I still battle to maintain a healthy mindset, but I am taking small steps with Jesus, and that's all that matters. I still have days when I look in the mirror and tell myself horrible things. But I experience more days when I choose to remind myself how much God loves me which allows me to love myself.

The other weekend I found myself at a twenty-first birthday party for one of the girls I lead. The girls that were there are the most genuine and loving people I have ever met.

We just hung out, ate amazing tacos, and talked.

While we were chatting it up, one girl complimented one of my friends about how perfect her body is. Flat stomach, perfect legs. You name it, and she had it. That started a conversation that stuck with me. While these girls were generous with their compliments, if they received one in return, they dismissed it. "Oh no, I do *not* have good legs. Look at yours!" "Have you seen my bulging stomach?" "If you think *you're* fat, you should look at me!"

These words, this language, broke me. Not only was I doing my fair share in participating in this conversation, but in my head I felt like I would never be able to accept the way my stomach looks and how my body is. These girls were beautiful, and I felt as if I was the one who stood out as clearly flawed. We were pulled into a hole of comparison with each other.

Here's the thing. Whether you are ninety pounds, four hundred pounds, or anywhere, below, above or in between, you are beautiful. 1 Peter 3:3-4 says "Your beauty should not come from outward adornment, such as elaborate hairstyles and the wearing of gold jewelry or fine clothes. Rather, it should be that of your inner self, the unfading beauty of a gentle and quiet spirit, which is of great worth in God's sight." We all have flaws and could probably name dozens of things we don't like about ourselves.

But let me tell you that God has made you for a reason and wants you to see yourself how he sees you. Every time you think of something negative about yourself, control your next thought and combat it with what God thinks about you.

Relying on God in helping you love yourself is critical. He is the definition of love, and when you get closer to the Lord, he defines you, he comforts you, and he reminds you of your purpose, your beauty, and why you are beautiful. He loves you. The creator of the universe loves you, so how could *you* not love you?

Proverbs 31:30 reminds us that "charm is deceptive, and beauty is fleeting; but a woman who fears the LORD is to be praised."

JESUS LOVES YOU MORE THAN YOU CAN FATHOM

It took a while to engrave in my head the truths that Jesus says about me. I have a sheet of paper that I got from a conference that has stuck with me to this day. I encourage you to remind yourselves how Jesus looks at you and the truths that we need to remember over the lies we believe:

1. You are not alone. (Hebrews 13:5)

2. You are promised a full life. (John 10:10)

3. You are a light to this world. (Matthew 5:14)

4. You are fearfully and wonderfully made. (Psalm 139:14)

5. You are forgiven. (Ephesians 1:7)

6. You are no longer a slave to sin. (Romans 8:1)

7. You are free. (Galatians 5:1)

8. You are a daughter of God. (John 1:12)

9. You are a co-heir to all of God's kingdom. (Romans 8:17)

10. You are loved forever. (Psalm 103:17)

11. You are welcomed by God. (Matthew 11:28)

12. You are chosen. (Ephesians 1:4)

13. You are taken care of by God. (Philippians 4:19)

14. You are secure. (Job 11:18)

15. You have hope. (Ephesians 1:12)

16. You have a purpose. (Psalm 57:2)

17. You have strength. (Ephesians 6:10)

18. You have been redeemed. (Romans 3:24)

Take a picture of these truths and put it as the background of your phone, or write one of these verses down and hang it up somewhere. Engrave these truths in your mind! Fight the lies and remember how God looks at you and why loving yourself is important.

While the COVID-19 pandemic and the stay-at-home orders were happening, I struggled with my body appearance more than ever before. My mom is an absolute ten out of ten. She truly resembles Jennifer Aniston. This is a prime example of how you can have the perfect body, perfect personally, and still struggle with your body image. Growing up, my mom would always talk negatively about herself. When I witnessed my mom speaking these things about her body, I couldn't help thinking about my own body. If my mom is drop-dead gorgeous and has a poor body image, how am I supposed to love my body?

As I mentioned earlier, I don't like my stomach and feel like I weigh probably twenty pounds more than I actually do. I realize now how this kind of mindset allowed me to develop an eating disorder. This issue only increased during my time locked in my house. I was constantly counting my calories, and if I had a sweet, then guilt and shame flooded me.

It led me to a path of destruction. I forced myself to throw up countless times. I had done this only a couple of times in the past, but it increased during the time of being isolated. It felt like that was the only thing I could control in my life since everything else around me was falling apart.

I was unhappy with my body and unhappy with myself. I was so focused on my outside appearance and the media and people around me that I totally forgot what God thought about me. God reminded me to focus on my inner beauty and heart than focusing on my outward appearance. This beautiful application has been the most life-changing experience. Accepting the grace and love the Lord has given me has allowed me to love every part of myself and transformed my character.

The best things I did to break up the negative thoughts and behaviors were: 1) to dive deeper into my past to figure out what lies I was believing, and 2) to examine the false messages my parents received and unintentionally instilled upon me.

WE ARE WORTHY OF LOVE (EVEN IF WE DON'T LOVE ALL OUR THOUGHTS OR CHOICES)

During my time of learning the love of God, I went to counseling, worked through some of my past issues, and took time to process and heal. There were certain things in my past that were kept in the dark that I never wanted to bring into the light.

Things grow and fester in the dark. John 11:20 says "It is when a person walks at night that they stumble, for they have no light."

Even deciding to put certain stories in this book brings up a lot of pain. I feel exposed knowing you will read my story on these pages. But I believe my pain and the hard things I have experienced are going to encourage others, bring people to repentance, and remind them that they can love themselves exactly as they are now.

In order to move forward, I first had to step back. I had to learn about my past and why I felt certain things. I learned that I didn't feel seen from the very beginning. This was a pattern in my life that started at a young age. One instance was when I started going to church with my childhood best friend who lived in my neighborhood. I walked into the church in fourth grade after not attending for the two years prior, and someone

I had met thousands of times walked up to me and asked my name.

Another moment in my childhood that has affected me happened when I was in elementary school. For a while, I honestly thought it was a dream. But as I got older, I realized it was a memory I wanted to block out of my mind. Through a Christian therapy approach called Splankna, I found out I was eight years old when I witnessed an event that brought me shame and guilt.

I was at my friend's house where we played the "closet game" with a group of Christian friends. I didn't participate in this act, but I witnessed each child go into the closet with another kid of the same-sex and participate in (what was assumed to be) sexual acts. Later that year at the same house my best friend and I ended up quickly kissing each other.

Although I don't remember anything else, I have come to learn that these experiences of me not knowing any better led me to believe countless lies. The devil had put so much shame and negative thoughts in my mind that I felt like I could never receive the love that God gives. In fact, I hated myself so much. It even led me to cutting my wrists because of the shame and guilt I felt. But these things that happened when I was a little kid were not my fault.

The things that happen in your childhood, my friend, were out of your control, and are not your fault. Because of the sin in this world, it has allowed the enemy to ruin what God intended this world to be. Genesis 50:20-21 says "You intended to harm me, but God intended it for good to accomplish what is now being done, the saving of many lives. So then, don't be afraid. I will provide for you and your children. And he reassured them and spoke kindly to them."

These childhood experiences led me to hide. It allowed me to never open up to my family about what had happened because I was fearful of what their response would have been. I was fearful of anyone finding out what had happened, so I kept it a secret and took it upon myself to carry the weight. When in reality, my parents would have welcomed me with open arms and loved me.

Around six years later, a movie came on TV that had a scene where two girls were kissing. Watching this sparked something inside of me that I didn't want to fully ignite. I didn't want to feel remotely turned on, but I did. I was so frustrated and mad and shameful that I ran from God for the longest time in middle school and the beginning of high school.

"God, why did this experience have to happen to me?" "Why did I have to go through these things?" "Why does this have to happen?" "I don't want to be attracted to girls." I brought God all of these questions and frustrations.

These lies started coming into my head at the same time as I became addicted to masturbation. This confusing mix of thoughts and actions shamed me all throughout high school. This struggle was something that I didn't think anyone related to, especially any girls. I thought I was alone in my feelings and didn't think anyone else could relate to me. But that is exactly what the devil wants us to believe.

I finally decided to open up to a few people about my experiences in the past and came to find out that those people had experienced something similar. At that moment, I knew that I wasn't alone and I wasn't some awful person. I knew I was loved by God and God was hurting with me in the mix of my struggle with lust and masturbation.

The fact is, I am attracted to boys, and I am looking forward to marrying the guy of my dreams someday. The devil's lies got in my head and caused me to believe that this was never going to happen because I have struggled with the experience of being lustful over the same-sex. We are sexual beings, and those same-sex feelings are more normal among others than we'd think. Because of what I had been exposed to at a young age, I thought I was alone. I didn't think I could ever tell anyone that, especially Christian people. I believe that some of you reading this are going through something similar too. Maybe you don't think you are loved or forgiven and feel like you are messed up. Read this: You are loved and washed by the blood of Jesus no matter what has happened! Hebrews 9:14 says, "How much more, then, will the blood of Christ,

You are loved and washed by the blood of Jesus.

who through the eternal Spirit offered himself unblemished to
God, cleanse our consciences from acts that lead to death, so
that we may serve the living God!" You are hidden in Christ,
and God sees you as no less, as referred in Colossians 3:3.

NOTHING WE DO CAN MAKE GOD LOVE US LESS

Maybe you even feel like if you opened up about these
things that the church would disown you. Or maybe you have
opened up about these things and your church, family, or friends
did disown you. Maybe these experiences have led you to run
away from God.

But whoever you are, whatever you have done, please know
that you are seen, my friend. You are loved and you are valued.
You are not eternally broken. God could never hate you, he hates
sin. He loves you so dearly. You are a child of God; he wants to
protect and redeem the things from your past experiences that
were out of your control. He wants to comfort you and remind
you that no matter how much you continue to mess up or think
those thoughts, you are loved and forgiven. Romans 5:8 says
"But God demonstrates his own love for us in this: While we
were still sinners, Christ died for us."

Jesus came for people like you and me.

He came for those who are caught up in sin. He wants to
bring us out of that sin and redeem us and love us exactly where
we are. I encourage you to open up to at least one other person
because, chances are, someone probably feels the same way you

do. Not ready for that yet? Feel free to shoot me an email or a DM on Instagram confessing this sin. My contact info is in the back of this book. Expressing yourself will encourage others to open up to you too. God created you for a purpose. Yes, there is sin in this world, but God can bring you out of it and use you for his purposes.

If you have opened up about same-sex attraction or an experience that has happened in your life before and people only brought you shame and guilt or disowned you, I am deeply sorry.

That is the response of broken, imperfect people.

That is not who Jesus is.

God wants to love you right where you are. Even if you have been or currently are involved in a same-sex relationship, God loves you. I encourage you to ask and allow God to transform your heart and to see what he sees. He will help you because he wants to protect you from the wounds of living in sin. The culture we live in and the truths of God doesn't always align, and that is a good thing.

Friend, *sin* doesn't make us *bad*. *Sin* makes us *dead*. Jesus didn't come to make us *good*; he came to bring us to *life*. God wants to set us free. Free from shame, free from guilt. God is a good, good God.

I'll be the first to admit that asking him to empower us to say no to sin—and accepting his forgiveness when we do sin—isn't always easy. But it is so worth it. I'm choosing to follow

Jesus and not give into sin because Jesus is so much greater than anything the world tries to seduce us with, and I trust that the Bible is our authority.

This life is not our own. 1 Corinthians 6:19-20 states, "Do you not know that your bodies are temples of the Holy Spirit, who is in you, whom you have received from God? You are not your own; you were bought at a price. Therefore honor God with your bodies."

Satan wants us to believe that we're not loveable. That we'll never be worthy. That the only way to quell the self-loathing is to embrace the temporary distractions of a lifestyle of sin.

I want to end this chapter by sharing with you two verses that remind me of the truth and help me combat Satan's lies. I hope they do the same for you:

"Then he said to all: 'Whoever wants to be my disciple must deny themselves and take up their cross daily and follow me'" (Luke 9:23).

"I have been crucified with Christ and I no longer live, but Christ lives in me. The life I now live in the body I live by faith in the Son of God, who loved me and gave himself for me" (Galatians 2:20). God loves you. God loves you because of who he is. When we start doubting God and who he is, we tend to start focusing our eyes on ourselves rather than focusing on him. We look at our guilt, shame, sins, and insecurities. Take your eyes off of yourself and focus on our loving God.

MADDIE'S STORY

Life is tough. We have hopes, expectations, and dreams that reality can sometimes turn into heartbreak, disappointment, and nightmares. We've all been there. The question to ask is, what are you going to do when things aren't going your way? Or when the worst-case scenario happens?

One of the ways Jesus has captured my heart is through my health. I was born with a heart defect that called for open-heart surgery at eleven days old and biannual visits to the cardiologist since. Fast forward a decade, a doctor told me I have Turner's Syndrome, which meant the chance of having my own kids is slim to nonexistent. Hard news to hear at any age, much less at age seventeen! However, through these experiences and others, Jesus continually reminds me that he is enough.

I could easily allow my health to define me and become chronically afraid of the future. I am not going to say I haven't done that. However, in the midst, Jesus is real. He is there. He is security. He satisfies. I am thankful to find my identity in the only One who can quench any thirst and fulfill any desire.

I encourage you to lean into the consistency of Jesus' character. When you don't understand your circumstances, turn to Jesus. When the future is filled with uncertainty, turn to Jesus. When you need rest, turn to Jesus. You will never regret it.

"The LORD will guide you always;
he will satisfy your needs in a sun-scorched land
and will strengthen your frame.
You will be like a well-watered garden,
like a spring whose waters never fail."
Isaiah 58:11

I follow Jesus because he is the only one who satisfies the deepest parts of my soul.

Learn more about how much God deeply loves us through Jesus' death on the cross. John 3:16-21, John 6:38, John 16:27, Jude 1:21, Psalm 109:26, Titus 3:5

——— REFLECTION QUESTIONS ———

1. Why should I love myself?

2. What qualities do I love about myself?

3. Why should I open up to people about the dark places in my life?

4. Why is it important to bring the darkness into light?

5. Why does Jesus tell us to carry our cross and follow him?

6. How can you trust the bible has authority?

CHAPTER 7

THE POWER OF YOUR TONGUE

Why Do Your Words Matter?

When I was in high school, I said some ignorant things. I didn't personally have an issue with cussing, however, throughout the last four years of being obedient, I have learned the value of choosing my words more carefully and guarding what I say.

Now, let me remind us here that our words—and any regrets we have of things we've said in the past (or even today!)—do not define us. We are defined by our identity as children of God.

That said, there have been plenty of times when I've said something insensitive and rude without thinking, then, later that day, find myself in deep regret. To this day, I look back on things I have said and cringe at the words that have come out of my mouth.

There have also been times where I have laughed or said terrible things about people—including those with disabilities, transgenders, people who are different than I am, random strangers on the street, and even friends—that I have later regretted. I looked at what I perceived to be flaws in these people while my own heart was broken and screwed up.

Check your heart. What is your heart saying? Usually, the words that come out of your mouth channel a deeper place in your heart. Pride, insecurities, hurt, lust, and people-pleasing are only a few areas of sin impacting your heart and creating an issue with your words. James 3: 9-11 says, "With the tongue we praise our Lord and Father, and with it we curse human beings, who have been made in God's likeness. Out of the same mouth come praise and cursing. My brothers and sisters, this should not be. Can both fresh water and salt water flow from the same spring? My brothers and sisters, can a fig tree bear olives, or a grapevine bear figs? Neither can a salt spring produce fresh water."

STICKS, STONES, AND WORDS CAN DO DAMAGE

I bought a season pass during the pandemic to hit the slopes every weekend since there wasn't anything else to do. Every time I would go skiing, I would sharpen more of my skills and develop greater confidence. One day, I was sitting on the ski lift with a friend who suggested skiing with some mutual friends. I responded, "Honestly, I would rather not ski with them because I don't want to be stuck on the bunny hills all day."

I felt convicted later. I thought about how our mutual friends would have felt if they'd heard those words. I realized my response was rooted in pride. It all came from a place of too much confidence and pride that it allowed me to not even consider skiing with people who had a lower skill set than me.

That experience showed me I was starting to look down upon others and judge them in my mind. That's why it is important to check your heart through your words because chances are there is something deeper going on. Ephesians 4:29 encourages us, "Do not let any unwholesome talk come out of your mouths, but only what is helpful for building others up according to their needs, that it may benefit those who listen."

Don't let your pride and other sin struggles that people have called you out on allow you to isolate yourself from the church and trusted Christian friends. Repent, apologize, and get on your knees to ask for forgiveness from our heavenly Father. If you don't feel the need to do that, pray to have a deep fear of God so that you can see his power.

We are powerless without the love of God. We need to humble ourselves and get on our knees.

We have to get to a place to know who God is and who we are in order to move forward in humility. Ever been on an airplane? When you look down, you see how tiny houses and cars look. Friend, from a plane, you can barely see a person. We are powerless without the love of God. We need to humble ourselves and get on our knees (2 Chronicles 7:14).

WE CAN BULLY PEOPLE WITH OUR WORDS

I remember another experience, but this memory is from middle school. In my math class, there was a nerdy kid who sat in the back of the class. After the bell rang, I saw he was reading his Bible. I walked to the back of the class and told him I thought it was cool he was reading his Bible. He got excited and started sharing with me things he was learning.

"What is your favorite Bible verse?" he asked.

Just then, I looked over and saw all my friends staring at us.

My pride kicked in, and I knew I needed to get away from this kid as quickly as possible. How did I get out of the conversation I started?

I rolled my eyes at his question.

"Probably John 3:16, I don't know," I said dismissively before leaving with my friends.

My insecurities and pride allowed me to treat that kid horribly to try to make myself look cool in front of my friends. I wonder how many times I have treated someone else as less than in order to make myself look cool. Probably way more times than I'd like to think. In fact, chances are we've all played the bully at some time in our life, perhaps even without realizing it.

Have you ever been on the other side and been the victim? Being that person doesn't feel good. Words can hurt, right? We've all been wounded by the words of others. It reminds me of the Bible story of the woman caught in adultery (John 8:1-11). A crowd of people were humiliating this woman because of her sin. Jesus reminded all of the entitled bullies that they had sinned too.

Have your words been unkind? Have you bullied others? Do you feel entitled?

Don't live in regret. Don't believe the lies that this is who you are or that you can't change.

There is hope for all of us.

Jesus was mocked and ridiculed, beaten and spit upon. And when you think about it, that could have been you or me spitting on him. And yet, Jesus loved those who bullied him. He loves all of *us*. In fact, he loves us so much that when we were still sinners, God chose us. "But God demonstrates his own love for us in this: While we were still sinners, Christ died for us" (Romans 5:8).

Through Jesus' sacrificial death for us on the cross, we can embrace hope and life. We can receive forgiveness. We can be empowered to see and love others; because he sees and loves us (1 John 4:12).

GOSSIP ISN'T CUTE OR FUNNY

If you're like me, you've been on both sides of the gossip coin—and neither is a good place to be. Talking about other people and getting talked about is an endless and dangerous cycle that I have personally experienced many times. I lived in a sorority house filled with thirty young women. That is the gateway drug of gossip.

Many times, I've been stuck in a conversation and walked away feeling disgusted. I didn't even need to *say* the terrible words—just listening to them—and I felt terrible.

And no wonder. When we gossip or listen to gossip, we're disrespecting people God created for a purpose. People God loves. People God wants to love through us. Are you spending time with the Lord? If we aren't, we are going to talk more like the world does not how Jesus does.

While working at my big-girl job, I was placed into an office with three amazing women. But fill a room with four girls, and it can get dangerous.

Every day I would walk into the office and hear two of the girls talking smack about someone else. It led to disappointment and sadness for the people they were talking about. Even just listening to these conversations without joining in made me feel sick. I wanted to speak up and defend the people being gossiped about. I remember thinking, *If I had the courage to stick up for someone, what kind of impact could that have? Could it make darkness flee, allow light to flow, and change a life?*

But then I argued myself out of doing the right thing. I justified my inaction by telling myself that these women were older than me, so they probably wouldn't listen to me anyway.

However, 1 Timothy 4:12 says otherwise, "Don't let anyone look down on you because you are young, but set an example for the believers in speech, in conduct, in love, in faith and in purity."

Now I know that second-guessing how others will respond isn't an excuse for not doing the right thing. Besides, when I stand up for my beliefs and let Jesus guide my moral compass, I'm not doing it alone. And neither are you. We have God right by our side the whole time.

Praying for the courage for God to help us intervene during gossipy conversations is a step in the right direction. Choosing not to participate in gossip—and even speaking out against it—increases trust, empowers healthier relationships, and demonstrates the love of Jesus.

You'll be amazed how freeing it will feel when you say *no* to speaking gossip or listening to it.

So, what kind of words and thoughts will we speak and entertain instead? As we pay attention to the power of our words to do harm, let's think about the power of our words to do good.

I'm providing a list of seven ways to bless someone with words instead of choosing gossip:

1. Know your friend's love language and speak to them through the following methods: words of affirmation, receiving gifts, acts of service, quality time, and physical touch.

2. Pray over them in person, or intentionally pray for them in your personal time.

3. Encourage them with quotes, sermons, or through
   Scripture.

4. Listen to them, and ask deep questions about their life.

5. Speak life into them, and call out the lies they are
   believing.

6. Compliment their character traits that come from Jesus
   that you love and admire.

7. Speak truth in their lives with grace. (Calling out sin can
   be hard to hear, but it's better to bring forth life than
   encourage death.)

My friend Katelyn has some great suggestions for using
words to give life—not death—to others:

KATELYN'S STORY

I remember times in my life when I have been deeply hurt
by the words of others. I can also remember times when I've
been the one saying hurtful things. In high school and college, I
have been both the perpetrator and the recipient of gossip.

I used to try to brush off the things others said about me,
but the truth is that words aren't easily erased. They carry a deeper significance than I have ever realized. They can be used to
hurt, belittle, demotivate, and demean. They can also be used to
praise, love, teach, inspire, and bestow value.

This realization has caused me to reevaluate how I speak
about others. I've also become more aware of the power of words

themselves. In Proverbs 13:3, the Lord reminds me that "those who guard their lips preserve their lives, but those who speak rashly will come to ruin." Ultimately, we are the only ones who have control over what we say, and knowing that words carry weight, we should use our words in a way that praises and glorifies God.

Today, I put a lot more thought into the things I say. A verse I have been working to memorize is James 1:19, which says, "My dear brothers and sisters, take note of this: Everyone should be quick to listen, slow to speak and slow to become angry." This verse reminds me to be thoughtful, understanding, and loving when using my words.

And you know what? This doesn't just apply to the words I speak to other people. It applies to the words I say to myself too. I am definitely hard on myself, and sometimes the words I speak to myself are not uplifting. When I say things to myself like, "I'm annoying" or "I don't look good" or "I'm not good enough," my words are damaging not only to me but also to God. I think it is important to keep in mind the things that God says about us; ultimately, those words are the only ones that matter.

I am the Lord's creation, and I want to dedicate my life to praising God and doing whatever I can to glorify him. Psalm 139:14 affirms my identity in Christ and his love for me: "I praise you because I am fearfully and wonderfully made; your works are wonderful, I know that full well." I follow Jesus because his words give me hope and a purpose.

Learn more about gossip and the power of your tongue through the wisdom that King Solomon- the wisest and foolish man that ever lived- gives. Proverbs 11:13, Proverbs 16:28, Proverbs 26:20, Proverbs 31:27

─── REFLECTION QUESTIONS ───

1. Why does God say I should be kind in my words?

2. What does the Bible say about the power of my tongue and why is it important to watch my speech?

3. How have I hurt others by my words and actions? Have I let that define who I am?

4. Why should I not gossip?

CHAPTER 8

GUT FEELINGS

Why Follow the Leadings of the Holy Spirit?

🦋

id you know that God can speak to you through your emotions and thoughts? While they can lead us astray at times, they can also lead us to incredible places that God wants us to be. Confusing, right? So how can we tell the difference?

The Bible is the compass we should follow. If an emotion is linked to a thought—or motivating you to an action—that doesn't match up to the truth of Scripture, don't follow it. But if your thoughts or feelings are guiding you in a direction that lines up with God's heart as revealed in Scripture, prayerfully let them lead you!

I want to share with you three experiences in which God used my thoughts and emotions in amazing ways.

HE NUDGES US THROUGH SEEMINGLY RANDOM THOUGHTS

Have you ever thought about how a simple text can impact someone's walk with Jesus? Checking up on your friends and family, and even paying attention to strangers, can encourage them, save them, and maybe even allow them to experience the love of Christ.

You may think that when someone crosses your mind, it's just a random thought. But have you considered that the Holy Spirit may be prompting you to reach out? It took me a while to learn how to pay attention to those "random thoughts" and respond by reaching out to people. One time I heard a song and texted the link to my high school Bible study group. Later, one girl told me that was exactly what she needed to hear at that very moment.

I don't know about you, but when someone sends me a song or a playlist, it is truly the way to my heart. It means someone thought about me. Since people started encouraging me through songs, I now use the same approach to reach out to others. Songs can be powerful. Whether it's a Christian song that exposes our heartstrings and brings on tears, or an upbeat, mood-boosting one, music has the power to bring out joy, happiness, and love.

HE CAN GUIDE US THROUGH DISCOMFORT

I had another gut feeling while leading a college Christian worship night at a frat house. As people were playing games and messing around, I felt an overwhelming feeling in my spirit to make sure we were not distracted from worship that night. I felt the strong urge to change the vibe of the room by blasting some worship music.

I didn't want to do it. It wasn't a comfortable thing to do. It felt awkward. But as I cranked up my house church playlist on Spotify, people began to pay attention. They began to worship and glorify God. The Holy Spirit overcame me as I privately and silently prayed over everyone in the room and asked the Holy Spirit to guide my words.

During the end of the worship night, I felt that there was someone we needed to pray for in the room. I asked if there was anyone who needed prayer. After an awkward moment of silence, a young man with tears in their eyes shared that he was struggling with certain areas of letting go of control. As we prayed over this person, I was so glad I had followed all that the Holy Spirit was leading me to do. God loves all of his people and can use us to show his love and care.

HE CAN LEAD US TO PRAY PASSIONATELY FOR OTHERS

One day I felt overly depressed. I could barely breathe from the amount of anxiety that I was feeling. I isolated myself in my room and put my head in the palms of my hands and felt extreme frustration. I didn't know how to cope with these feelings.

I started to pray even though it was a hard thing to do. I had to force myself to talk to God at that point. Eventually, I stopped talking and sat in silence with God, trusting that he knew my thoughts and feelings.

As I sat in frustration and despair, God spoke a name to me. This random guy from high school popped in my mind, and I felt the need to pray over him. God impressed on me the thought that the frustration and despair I felt were exactly what this high school friend had been feeling that day.

As soon as I took God out of the box, I had put him in and actively listened to his prompting, it allowed him to work in miraculous ways. I decided to text the guy that popped in my mind and encourage him. The words weren't coming from me. I knew they were coming from the power of Jesus working inside me.

He responded about five hours later and said he was in complete shock over how my message to him had hit home. He told me he needed to hear the truths of Scripture and encouraging words.

A couple of months later, I asked him what had happened that day. He told me that he had been reeling with anger, frustration, and despair over learning that his dad, who was a recovering alcoholic, had relapsed.

There is no way I would have known that. But God used my own emotions to prompt me to intervene passionately for a struggling friend.

God works in ways that I can't even put into words.

After this experience, this friend and I shared memories to-gether over the phone, on walks, and on long drives. We talked about Jesus and the wonders of God's miracles. We spent hours in the car talking all about our lives and how Jesus has impacted us.

His faith was one I can't even put into words. He had a gift of discernment and would love people so deeply. He could read you like a book and carried the burdens of his family and friends daily.

He would tell me how much he wanted Jesus to come back and how our lives are not meant for this world, but for heaven and life with Jesus. He lived daily with this mindset.

About a year later, after this experience and sharing these memories with him, he was in a tragic boating wreck in which his body went missing. His body was found three days later on a Sunday. His death even pointed to Jesus. Three days later Jesus rose from the dead. 1 Corinthians 15:4 says, "He was buried . . . he was raised on the third day according to the Scriptures."

God had given me that prompting a year before his death for a reason. That prompting from the Holy Spirit allowed me to know my friend so deeply a year before he passed and to know Jesus on a deeper level. He has truly made an impact in this world and in the kingdom of heaven.

One of the last texts I received from my friend was this:

> We all have been places where we are uncomfortable. There is a saying that I live by the saying, "Be comfortable with the uncomfortable." When you settle in a place you don't grow. Being uncomfortable allows you to discover things you didn't know about yourself.

> You drive to become a better person, not just for you, but for the Lord. I believe God is the God of miracles. He made the blind see and the dead walk. What you are going through, he will deliver you to peace and a calm heart. I pray you lead others to see how small their problems are because Christ is so large and moving.

SOMETIMES HE'S NUDGING YOU TO RECEIVE HELP, ENCOURAGEMENT, OR COMFORT

I've been sharing about following the leading of the Holy Spirit when he wants you to minister to others. But the flip side is that sometimes God will lead others to minister to you. Can you anticipate, recognize, and surrender to that kind of blessing in your life?

A couple of months ago, my friend Rachel was having a graduation party. The morning of her party, I saw a yellow butterfly. I had a feeling that God had something special planned for me that night.

Turns out, God did what he said he would.

Being on the stubborn side, I typically try to do things on my own. I may seek council from friends but never from older women. It feels intimidating to me for some reason. But that night, I talked to Rachel's grandma for three hours. I had been yearning to talk to someone who had been successfully married for over fifty years, and she was an answer to that prayer. She shared great wisdom with me. She told me the story of her decades-long marriage and answered all of my questions about the secrets to having a healthy, godly union that will last.

God is the God of miracles

Here are some highlights from our talk:

- "My marriage is a revolving door. Every time we want to leave, God brings us right back together."
- "In every circumstance, go back to Jesus. He brings people together."
- "I thought I was a strong, independent woman and didn't need a man. But throughout our marriage, I realized we were stronger together. We have overcome cancer and job loss together. Life is better with him in it."

- "Laughter is important. When you spend years
  with someone, you need to have fun with them."

As I drove home that night, I bawled. God knew I needed
her to speak wisdom in my life. I saw a yellow butterfly again
several weeks later and immediately felt that God had another
special moment planned for me. (I love how God brings me
signs and wonders throughout the day!)

I went to my friend's wedding on a random Thursday
night. God placed me at the same table as my pastor's wife. Immediately, I knew she was going to be an answered prayer. We
were both moved by our conversation, recognizing that our time
together had been ordained by God. She encouraged me to go
to counseling. She shared how Eye Movement Desensitization
and Reprocessing (EMDR) and Splankna has impacted her life
and the lives of others. She also encouraged me to write this
book. She spoke wisdom into my life regarding mental health
and how it impacts our walk with God.

After this conversation, I spent the drive back home wor-
shiping God for all of his goodness—I even was encouraged to
start going to therapy. God knew I needed her to speak wisdom
into my life.

HE CAN COMFORT US THROUGH OUR OWN EMOTIONS

The Bible tells a story about Jesus and his disciples in a boat
on a very stormy sea. While Jesus was sleeping, his disciples were

screaming and freaking out because the world was going crazy around them.

The truth is that sometimes our circumstances are scary. Sometimes God comforts us through his word, asking us to believe him and trust him even when our emotions are painfully raging within us. Sometimes, however, he comforts us with supernatural feelings of joy and peace, like in Eboni's story below.

EBONI'S STORY

I've experienced in my life an overwhelming joy and peace I have never felt before. It all started in church. I was praising God while streams of tears rolled down my face and my hands were raised toward the ceiling in surrender. I was surrounded by believers who worship the same God with all their heart, soul, and might. The joy I felt was indescribable, the presence of God that took over the service was unmatched with greatness.

Ever since that day, I surrendered my life to finding every opportunity I could to give to others, whether that was a smile or praying for someone at a grocery store. We are here to love people like Christ loves us. It says in 1 John 4:11, "Dear friends, since God so loved us, we also ought to love one another, No one has even seen God; but if we love one another, God lives in us and his love is made complete in us." God tells us that we need to love one another. If God calls me to do so, then I want to share the love of God abroad so others can express the love of God. I know it's not me who loves; it's God in me.

In my life I've dealt with homelessness in the form of not having a permanent address in my high school years and going into college. Even through these circumstances, I felt the joy and the peace of God. Sometimes my circumstances became an adventure because I felt God's watchful presence. I know in the future that no matter what situation I'm in, I can count on the presence of God's joy and peace in my life. I follow Jesus because I want to live a life of being surrounded by his joy, peace, and presence. Even when I'm in the valley, I know I'm able to call upon his name.

Learn more about the leading of the Holy Spirit throughout the scripture. Acts 2:1-4, Acts 2:38, Acts 4, Acts 16:16-40 Luke 11:13

——— REFLECTION QUESTIONS ———

1. Do you experience thoughts, feelings, promptings, or urgings that you think are not from the Holy Spirit? How can you tell the difference?

2. If you're not sure how to discern God's voice, chat about it with a pastor, counselor, or godly friend who can help you figure out if these promptings are in line with God's truth or not. Write down the name of someone you could talk to, if needed.

3. Why should you listen to the Holy Spirit when it feels uncomfortable?

4. Describe an experience you've had accepting encouragement or wisdom from others. Was it difficult or easy for you to do so?

5. What is the Holy Spirit? Why should I trust him?

CHAPTER 9

THIS WORLD IS BROKEN

Why Should I Forgive?

*F*orgiveness. This is a subject I have always struggled with, whether we're talking about forgiving people who have hurt me, or forgiving myself for sinning or hurting others.

Let me begin with the simple fact that this world is messed up. People hurt people in the most horrific ways. My heart hurts thinking about how much pain people have gone through because of abuse, rape, deaths, lies, betrayal, divorce, and so many other different things.

Why should I forgive myself when I have messed up? Why should I forgive myself when I have struggled with the same sin repeatedly and continue to fall? Why should I forgive others when they have dug a wound so deep into my soul that I feel like I can never heal or recover from it? Why should I forgive someone when they hurt someone I love?

These are all valid questions and feelings. But the answer is *Jesus*. Jesus is why.

Scripture tells us, "For if you forgive other people when they sin against you, your heavenly father will also forgive you" (Matthew 6:14).

In other words, forgiveness is the heart of Christianity.

GOD FORGIVES US

Think about it. God sent down *his Son* Jesus on the cross because this world was corrupt, sinful, and destructive. Jesus lived a perfect life and then died for *our sins*. He was the ultimate sacrifice once he rose again three days later, conquering death, and ushering in the ministry of the Holy Spirit, which brought about the forgiveness of our sins. God wants us to forgive ourselves and others, just as he has done.

Let's start with the challenge of forgiving ourselves. If you are struggling with forgiving yourself, begin with this prayer:

Jesus, I need you. I have done something that has allowed me to not be forgiving of myself. I am broken. I am a mess. I need you to help me restore my heart and cleanse my soul. You, Lord, sent your Son to the cross for my sins in order for me to be forgiven. You see me as perfect and don't look at me any less or any more.

My sins are wiped away because of you, Jesus. You, God, see me as holy because Jesus is in me. Thank you! I praise you, Lord. I pray you help me forgive myself. Set me free, Lord, from any bondage I have in this world. Set me free from my sin and mistakes, Lord.

Take away my shame; it is not from you. Thank you for always loving me and comforting me, even when it's hard to see the best in me. I repent. Jesus, we pray, Amen.

Don't be hard on yourself; this can take time. But it's worth it. When we wallow in our self-loathing and deny grace for ourselves, we remain in a hard place that can set us back in our faith. Be obedient and receive God's grace.

Romans 5:8 says, "But God demonstrates his own love for us in this: While we were still sinners, Christ died for us." In other words, while we were still destructive, rebellious, and wanting nothing to do with God, he continued to love us. And he continues to love us today. Let that sink in for a second. Think about every mistake, sin, and bad thing you have done and know that God has loved you from the very beginning. Not only does he love you, he can't love you any more or any less. He loves you right where you are at this very moment. How amazing is that?

My desire is to be so forgiving and loving to friends, family, and strangers that they get pointed to Jesus. That is only developed when God works inside of me. My pride would never allow me to forgive someone who has hurt me deeply. It takes an extreme amount of humility to be able to forgive others. Jesus' strength is the only way that I can forgive others.

Jesus' strength is the only way that we can forgive others.

THE PROCESS OF FORGIVING OTHERS CHANGES US

Sin—ours or the sins of others—brings brokenhearted-ness. Forgiveness is our way back to freedom.

The end of my sophomore year of college, I was picking weeds in an older couple's garden for community service hours my sorority has us do every year. The night before, I drank more than I should have and got myself into a bad situation. My heart was burdened and broken that morning. That same day, an ex-boyfriend I still had feelings for called me and confessed that he'd done something stupid and slept with a girl he'd had a thing with in the past.

We were broken up, so it's not like he had cheated on me. But it was clear in his voice how much he deeply cared about me. He was being the bigger person by humbling himself and confessing his sin to me.

I felt the Holy Spirit rush over me and take over in that moment. It was Jesus who gave me the strength to forgive him right on the spot. We are all sinful and make countless mistakes. In that moment, I looked at my ex-boyfriend in the way God saw him. He was broken and in shocked disbelief that he did something like that. His sinful nature got the best of him. His true nature is a child of God.

On the other hand, it took me years to forgive the girl he slept with. It even took me years to forgive myself. My insecurities and jealousy overcame me. Sometimes I ran into her at parties, and, honestly, I wanted to punch her in the face. There was one day that I almost punched her, but I knew that behavior wasn't godly. Thankfully, I came to my senses.

A year later, I walked into a class I was excited to take, saw that she was in the same class, and immediately, my entire body filled with rage. The self-control I had to have in that class was insane. I knew God allowed her to be in my class because I needed to forgive her and work on my heart and my bitterness and insecurities. I knew God wanted me to move forward. God led me to pray for her; in time, he helped me see her the way he sees her. Instead of rage, I began to feel compassion. Let me tell you, praying for your enemies is tough, but it will leave you free from the burden of bitterness, sadness, and anger. A year after that class, I ran into her at a country concert and was free from this anger and able to love her how God loves her. This was only possible with God (Matthew 19:26).

EVEN THOUGH FORGIVENESS TAKES TIME, IT'S WORTH IT

When I was a junior in high school, my parents divorced. It was an ugly one that left me in pain and heartbreak. It gave me a view of how marriage *isn't* supposed to be. In fact, after their divorce, I began to view marriage as an awful thing and didn't want to go anywhere near it.

The day after my dad had been served divorce papers, I was at Beau Jo's pizza after a hike in the mountains. My heart dropped as I got a call from my sister telling me that I needed to call my dad as soon as possible.

A few nights earlier, I'd gone looking for my dad when he wasn't answering our texts. I'd found him drunk, walking around. He'd hit the back of my car and was yelling and slurring his words.

And now this.

I stepped outside Beau Jo's to call my dad and saw that he had just texted my sister and me. He told us we needed to take care of our little brother, then said he was proud of the women we were today.

It sounded like a suicide note.

I called my dad right away. I told him I loved him and told him I wouldn't know what to do if he was gone. In the meantime, my mom had contacted my uncle, who had called 911. An ambulance arrived at my dad's house. Thankfully, he was okay and hadn't harmed himself.

The next day when he was in the hospital, I walked into our childhood home where he was still living, and the whole house was a mess. Broken plates, holes in the walls, food thrown everywhere, doors pulled off the hinges.

My heart broke. I knew that he was broken and deeply hurt, but I was still angry and mad at him for his actions.

Because of that, I didn't talk to my dad much the last couple of years of high school. He didn't show up to my prom pictures, and he didn't treat me the way he should have treated me throughout the remainder of high school. I even had to block his number from time to time.

It wasn't until four years later, during COVID-19, that I was able to restore our relationship and fully forgive him. Praise Jesus for that. I started praying for my dad and decided to forgive my dad for his actions. I prayed that God would give me a different view and a different perspective of him. I wanted to see my dad the way God, the Creator of the universe, saw him. As the Lord worked in my heart, I felt deep love for my dad, even through some of his choices had hurt me. My dad's actions don't define who he is. Jesus defines who he is. Jesus defines who we are.

We are all broken and messed-up people. that are in need of a savior. God sent Jesus into this world for our sins. Jesus forgives us first, so we are able to forgive others.

SKYLAR'S STORY

I am currently a senior in college and will be married in May. I want to share with you a piece of who I am, something I used to describe as a "piece of my past," but now I acknowledge it is a part of who I am. I was sexually abused by my father at a young age. I blocked out the experience for many years, unable to remember the specific events that had occurred.

During my late middle-school years, my father began to pursue a relationship with me that escalated into what I now know is called "grooming," which is a tactic used to build trust with a child with the intent of gaining alone time to do things I'd rather not define.

I realized all of this during a therapy session. Immediately following that appointment, the Department of Human Services got involved, removed him from my life, and began a court trial.

A few years after that, I was diagnosed with severe PTSD from the events that took place when I was a child and young woman. Needless to say, the events that destroyed my ability to experience life as an innocent young girl proceeded to change my entire life.

I was not a follower of Jesus while all of this was happening in my life. To be frank, I was not interested in believing in a God who would allow all these horrific things to happen to me. It wasn't until my freshman year of college that I was introduced to the unconditional love of God, love that led to him sending his one and only son to die for my sins and bridge the gap so I could have a personal, loving relationship with Jesus.

Upon learning that beautiful *good* news, I thought I could leave my painful past behind. I didn't think my relationship with God needed to include what happened to me when I was young. I also assumed my father had caused too much pain to have the same beautiful relationship with God that I had.

What I've learned throughout my three years of loving Jesus is something that is still hard for me to swallow sometimes today.

Romans 8:38–39 says, "For I am convinced that neither death nor life, neither angels nor demons, neither the present nor the future, nor any powers, neither height nor depth, nor anything else in all creation, will be able to separate us from the love of God that is in Christ Jesus our Lord." This verse brought so much comfort when I thought about God saying it to me. On the flip side, it brought up so much anger when I thought about him saying it to my father.

That's the thing about the God we love; he loves everybody else just as much as he loves us, even the people who cause us an immense amount of pain. That being said, he is also our protector and our defender. Part of his love for me is his hate for the sin used against me that almost destroyed me. I believe there will be justice brought to that one day, a type of justice that is out of my control.

But what God wants for me is freedom from my pain and bitterness. He wants freedom for me that can only be experienced as I learn to love my enemies. That was another hard pill for me to swallow. I once thought that in order to be free from my pain, my father had to be in jail or feel awful for what he did to me, both of which haven't occurred. In truth, freedom from my pain requires forgiveness—a word I never thought I would say in the same sentence as the word "dad."

Forgiveness is a lifelong process, one Jesus never intended for us to do alone. Whatever battle you are facing, whatever unjustified pain somebody caused you, God cares for you. He fights for you and your heart. What happened to you was not okay. God wants to take hold of you and love you in a way nobody else can.

Philippians 4:19 says, "And my God will meet all your needs according to the riches of his glory in Christ Jesus." My God will meet all my needs. He will meet my need to feel validated in my pain. He will meet my need to feel loved and cared for by a father. He will meet my need to move forward in life and be who I was created to be. Why do I follow Jesus? Because he loves me and demonstrated that love by giving his life for me. In turn, he encourages me to do the same for others.

Learn more about how Jesus displays forgiveness in scripture. John 8:1-20, Matthew 18:21-22, Genesis 45:4-8, John 23:33-34, Acts 7:58-60, 1 Samuel 24:1-15

REFLECTION QUESTIONS

1. Are you struggling to forgive yourself about a past or present sin?

2. Why do you think you are having a hard time forgiving yourself?

3. What are steps, changes, or things you can be doing to allow you to forgive yourself?

4. What does the Bible say about forgiveness?

5. Why is forgiveness a good thing even when it doesn't feel good?

6. Who are you not willing to forgive? Why?

7. Why should you forgive the person who hurt you?

8. Why is forgiveness of others important?

9. Why should I forgive the group of people who hurt me so deeply and embarrassed me?

10. How can I experience the forgiveness of God and believe forgiveness is a good thing?

CHAPTER 10

SOCIAL MEDIA

Why Honor God in Every Area of Life?

The addiction I have to Instagram is unfathomable. I simply cannot control myself from unlocking my phone and clicking on the bright pink Instagram icon. My drug of choice is social media.

Unfortunately, this "drug" has brought me anxiety and depression. On top of that, I've realized that my use of social media has not been God-honoring at all. In fact, it was leading me down a road toward destruction: spiritually, emotionally, and relationally.

SOCIAL MEDIA TEMPTS US TO ACT IN THE FLESH RATHER THAN WALK IN THE SPIRIT

Why are you on social media?

Is it to compete with others?

Is it to impress others?

Is it to try to be someone else?

Is it to fill time?

Is it to fill a void?

Or, are you wanting to encourage others by sharing the love of Jesus?

Most of my days, I am glued to my phone. There are rarely ever times when I am sitting outside enjoying the view, listening to the birds, or cooking a new meal. My hobbies have been snatched away from me because of just one device.

And I'm not the only one. Many of my friends are coming to the same realization. Maybe you are too.

Let me ask another question. If social media was God-honoring would we*:*

- *constantly be scrolling in comparison?*
- *constantly be wishing we were someone else?*
- *constantly be trying to fill a void?*

When I am on social media, I am drained. I get disappointed that I am not engaged, married, or have a kid yet. I get upset when someone has a better job than I do. I get angry. I get jealous. These feelings ultimately aren't from God at all. These aren't even the fruit of the Spirit. These feelings are from the flesh.

Look at what Galatians 5:16–26 has to say about our flesh versus walking in the Spirit:

"So I say, walk by the Spirit, and you will not gratify the desires of the flesh. For the flesh desires what is contrary to the Spirit, and the Spirit what is contrary to the flesh. They are in conflict with each other, so that you are not to do whatever you want. But if you are led by the Spirit, you are not under the law.

The acts of the flesh are obvious: sexual immorality, impurity and debauchery; idolatry and witchcraft; hatred, discord, jealousy, fits of rage, selfish ambition, dissensions, factions and envy; drunkenness, orgies, and the like. I warn you, as I did before, that those who live like this will not inherit the kingdom of God.

But the fruit of the Spirit is love, joy, peace, forbearance, kindness, goodness, faithfulness, gentleness and self-control. Against such things there is no law. Those who belong to Christ Jesus have crucified the flesh with its passions and desires. Since we live by the Spirit, let us keep in step with the Spirit. Let us not become conceited, provoking and envying each other."

Social media is a platform that entices you to act in the flesh rather than the spirit. If you are like me, knowing these truths convicted me.

FASTING FROM SOCIAL MEDIA REDUCES ANXIETY

We carry our addiction with us every single day in the palm of our hands. Some of us struggle with porn, comparison, or distraction. We need to normalize taking a break from the world being constantly shoved in our face and instead run toward the eternal perspective.

When I delete my social media apps off my phone, anxiety gets released. There's no one I am trying to impress and no one I'm comparing myself to. Fasting ultimately kills the flesh and allows the spirit to live.

Choosing to fast ultimately allows God to gain honor.

Choosing to fast ultimately allows God to gain honor. When we fast, we choose God over our desires of social media. This brings us freedom. Most of us are chained to our phones, and God wants to break us free from them.

WHEN WE'RE NOT DISTRACTED, WE CAN RESPOND TO WHAT GOD IS DOING IN OUR LIVES

Most of the time, when my life is impacted deeply by the peace of Jesus, it's off social media. When I was in high school, I took a break from my phone and went to the pool with my mom. While we were there, my brother's best friend's mom sat with us. As she was chatting with my mom, I overheard her talking about how her husband was a pastor and that they had youth group meetings on Thursday nights.

Youth group?

I jumped into the conversation. "Can I come?"

I had drifted far from God. I knew I was using social media to numb my pain, and I didn't know how to stop or where to go for real relief. I knew this was an opportunity that I couldn't pass up. I hid all my excitement and nervousness as she told me she would pick me up the next day to take me to the youth group.

This woman ended up being a mentor and role model in my life for a season. Three months to be exact. In those three months, she impacted my life in an extreme manner. She taught me that I was forgiven in my imperfections and my mistakes. She taught me that God was here with me in the midst of heartbreak. She brought me to a safe place that would be filled with fellowship and deep friendships.

She nurtured me under her wings in these three months and helped me to connect with others in a healthy way and build honorable relationships. Ultimately, she helped me build a foundation to pursue a perfect God—all while still being imperfect.

I was still smoking weed, having sex, and consumed by what everyone was thinking of me. This trajectory moment ultimately brought me to a community that convicted me to stop living in sin and start living a life completely for Jesus four years later.

Although it took time and didn't happen right away, being led by a godly mentor impacted my journey in the pursuit of holiness. This woman encouraged me and led me and had more of an impact on me than she probably even knows.

Five years later, when my brother gave his life to Christ, it was because this same family invited him to attend a Christian camp. How amazing is that?

God can work through one person and one family. And that one family can impact not only another family, but an entire generation in the process.

And just think—none of this might have happened if we had all been glued to our phones that day at the pool.

This is *why* putting your phone down is important.

When was the last time you turned off all your social media and just listened? To God? To people around you?

One day, while sitting in a coffee shop, I turned my phone and music off and just paid attention. The atmosphere in that shop seemed to completely change. Listening, I realized people at the table next to me were speaking truth about Jesus and his life.

Can you believe that his life is so beyond powerful that people still talk about Him today? Jesus is a debate to so many people, but his name is brought up over and over again in conversations and conversations.

When was the last time you prayed over someone or brought up Jesus' name in a simple conversation? When was the last time you sent a DM to someone and asked them about their life? Have you ever thought about how a small action, an invite, a prayer, or simply setting your phone down can bring life over someone around you in a miraculous way?

DELETING SOCIAL MEDIA FREES UP TIME FOR THINGS OF GREATER VALUE

How much more time would you have if you were off social media? What would you gain if you didn't have social media?

- Better relationships
- Improved skills and hobbies
- Less anxiety and depression
- More time with God

When we fill our hours with social media, the enemy gets excited. The enemy wants us to be distracted. He wants our attention and our thoughts to be consumed by this world.

When Jesus came into this world, he went to a solitary place to be near and talk to God. When am I solitary? When am I completely alone with God? Even in the moments before drifting into sleep, I am distracted. I can't even tell you the times that I've fallen asleep while scrolling on Instagram.

Have you ever been bothered when someone isn't listening to you because they are on their phone? One of my biggest pet peeves is when I am talking to someone and I look over and they are staring at their phone, scrolling or texting.

But that got me thinking. How many times do I do that to other people? Probably more often than I'd like to admit. I am so consumed by my phone that I am often unaware of my surroundings.

My current job is in marketing. That means part of my job is being on social media. I love artsy filters, editing on light room and VSCO, and making fun videos. I love having my feed aesthetically pleasing to look at.

But one day, I checked my heart and realized I had all the wrong motives:

1. I wanted others to be impressed by me.

2. I wanted to prove people wrong by being successful and doing cool things.

3. I wanted to feel good about myself.

These led into feeding the flesh. I was idolizing myself and trying to please people.

Galatians 1:10 hits it home with this one. "Am I now trying to win the approval of human beings, or of God? Or am I trying to please people? If I were still trying to please people, I would not be a servant of Christ."

Deleting social media would be tantamount to killing our flesh.

Do we dare?

NUHA'S STORY

I was raised in an Orthodox Christian household in an entirely different culture in America. Being raised under a different culture made me feel like I never fit in at church or school. Part of it could have been a lie and part of it could have been true. In this world, we were never meant to fit in.

Jesus made us uniquely different, and while we are all one family in God, it is our differences that strengthen us. However, growing up, it's hard to see the big picture. Throughout my childhood and into high school, I struggled with the concept of loving myself and who I am. My cultural background was a huge part of learning to love that part of me. I have always wanted to look "American" so Americans would like and accept me more. It was a difficult journey, but I learned to see the beauty of both cultures. It helps me understand people more, understand different cultures, and sympathize with what they go through. This is a gift Jesus gave me. I have to continue to remind myself about what Jesus would think of me.

He created us all in his image. Whenever I want to look like someone else, I feel like it is an insult to his creation. How cool is it that he never makes mistakes? He's incredible! He created the stars and this universe. Whenever I look around at this beautiful world, I see the beauty of its nature. But on the other hand, when I look at my phone all day, my view gets distorted. With social media, it triggers a constant comparison.

It can be hard to not be consumed by it and have your thoughts become negative about yourself. I struggle with this daily. However, Jesus has continued to help me with this struggle. He has taught me to grow and recognize the beauty that he sees in me through Scripture. Even though there are times when I feel skinny, I still feel like I am not enough. When I feel smart, I still don't feel smart enough.

No matter how I feel, I don't feel like I am beautiful enough, good enough for a guy, good enough for a friend, and the list goes on. But those are all lies! Sometimes it's hard to distinguish lies from truth, but when I have allowed Jesus in, he has helped me grow in his truth. I am not saying I don't struggle; I still do. I still get caught up in lies and comparison, but I take it day by day. I try to give it all to God. I am not always good at it, but I try.

I struggled with pleasing people because I thought I wasn't enough. I got caught up with looking through the lies and perspectives of the world, when the only perspective or opinion that truly matters is Jesus.

2 Corinthians 4:6 says, "For God, who said, 'Let light shine out of darkness,' made his light shine in our hearts to give us the light of the knowledge of God's glory displayed in the face of Christ."

Learn more about what the bible says about how we can honor God. Matthew 6:22-23, Psalm 119:37, 1 Peter 5:8-9, Proverbs 4:23, 1 Corinthians 10:31, 1 Corinthians 6:20, Colossians 3:17

─────── REFLECTION QUESTIONS ───────

1. Why is it important to limit myself on social media and overall screen time?

2. How can I glorify God through social media?

3. Why should I delete or fast from social media?

4. Why should I talk about Jesus to unbelievers on social media?

5. How can I stop comparing myself to others? Why is this important?

CHAPTER 11

RENEWING THE MIND
Why Keep Yourself Pure?

I lost my virginity a month before turning seventeen. It was the morning after a Zac Brown Band concert. Right after it happened, I was filled with so much shame, grief, and heartbreak. I drove home afterward and just cried and cried. But that didn't stop me in high school from continuing to sleep with my boyfriend.

I became numb. Numb to the truth that having sex outside of marriage was a sin. At a Christian camp, one of the leaders looked at me and said, "Please tell me you haven't had sex yet!" I lied in response to her because I felt judgement and shame. I forgot why God was telling me to not have sex and to be pure.

I thought purity was a joke. I thought it was normal to sleep with your boyfriend in high school. In fact, if you weren't, then you would be the odd one out. It had always been a con-

stant battle to remind myself why I shouldn't be getting drunk
and why I shouldn't be having sex.

As I've mentioned, I hate being told what to do. I find it
hard to get mentored or hear about the truths in the Bible coming from someone else's mouth.

Unfortunately, I typically have to discover why I shouldn't
be doing these things on my own.

SIN IS A LITTLE LIKE DOG VOMIT

In November 2020, I was house-sitting and dog-sitting
two adorable dogs for two weeks. I was pumped up to watch
a Goldendoodle and a Golden Retriever until I found out the
long list of duties required daily to maintain their upkeep, on
top of the upkeep of the house. I had to give these dogs pills in
the morning and at night. Walk them twice a day and clean up
poop in the backyard three to four times a week. Also, I had to
water the plants and keep up with the mail.

On top of that, I had to feed them, feed the cat, and clean
out the litter box. It's all fun and games until you have to do
the work, right? While this may not seem like a whole lot to
people, I had to work forty hours a week and attend a couple of
small groups through church multiple times a week. Needless to
say, it made me realize I am not meant to be a dog mom quite
yet.

The first day of house-sitting I was laying on the couch,
FaceTiming my mom. All of a sudden, the Golden Retriever

puked everywhere. I mean everywhere. To top it all off, there were chunks of poop in the vomit (yuck!). I didn't realize the seriousness of the owner telling me that the dog ate poop, but she was serious. Shortly after that, the Goldendoodle proceeded to vomit on me. I had to clean up this mess and about vomited in the process because of the terrible smell that went throughout the house. In this scenario, sin is like poop.

The Golden Retriever had no idea that the poop was bad for him; he just continued to eat it and eat it. He probably enjoyed it because every time he sees poop, he eats it. But in the end, his stomach felt terrible and he always threw it up. **The more we sin, the more numb we become to it and enjoy it.** Then, when we proceed to fall on our face and vomit after making countless mistakes and feeling empty inside, we realize that sin is not a good thing after all. Sin then can affect others around us to begin sinning with us. Proverbs 26:11 says, "As a dog returns to its vomit, so a fool repeats their folly."

God brings our brokenness and mistakes into redemption.

I look at the people I knew from high school and middle school who have dug a hole of spending too much time in sin, and my heart breaks for them. Most of them ended up in prison, are homeless, have broken marriages, had a kid before marriage, or became an alcoholic. Naming these things are never meant to bring shame but show that there are consequences to sin. However, God is a good God, and he redeems us. He brings our brokenness and mistakes into redemption.

Sin can be comfortable and feel good. Having sex outside of marriage and getting drunk feels good, especially when you know it's the wrong thing to do. People with a rebellious nature feed off of this. In my experience, these actions have always led me to mistakes, shame, and regret. Sin leads to destruction. Sex outside of marriage never brought me more joy; it brought me more pain. Getting drunk never brought me more joy; it brought me regret and heartache. Getting high never brought me more joy; it brought me increased depression, anxiety, and laziness.

GOD WANTS TO HELP US DO WHAT IS RIGHT

As I mentioned earlier, I got into a relationship in college, where I ended up having sex with my boyfriend. Little did I know I was in the same pattern that I was in high school.

I, then, stopped having sex the end of my sophomore year of college. It took me from my sophomore year of high school until my sophomore year of college to stop that sin and build godly habits instead. It's never too late to repent. And then repent again. And again, and again. And then run as fast as you can away from that sin.

1 Corinthians 10:13 says, "No temptation has overtaken you except what is common to mankind. And God is faithful; he will not let you be tempted beyond what you can bear. But

when you are tempted, he will also provide a way out so that you can endure it."

That Golden Retriever would see poop and eat it. Sometimes, the best way to not get caught in sin is to get rid of the temptation and have people around us to help us walk in purity and righteousness. I picked up that poop for the Golden Retriever and would go outside with him to make sure he didn't eat it again.

How did I pursue purity, you may ask? Definitely not gracefully, but I did it! I broke up with my college boyfriend shortly after we stopped having sex at the end of my sophomore year when I was at a discipleship Christian camp. About five months later, we got back together. We wanted to do it the right with purity this time, so we stopped having sex. We had to establish boundaries.

Establishing these boundaries was extremely hard. Let me tell you, when you cross the line, it's possible to cross that line again. Feelings can lead you astray, especially when you are just wanting to bring that feeling back again. It seems nearly impossible in that moment you're kissing and touching to try and go back to a pure mindset and remember why it's important to not have sex outside of marriage.

All of this seems hard to do, but we don't have to do it alone. There are choices we can make that invite the power of God to help us win the battle against temptation. Repentance, boundaries, accountability, friends who encourage us with scripture and prayer can help us change the patterns that Satan hopes will destroy us.

FOLLOWING GOD'S DESIGN BRINGS JOY AND PEACE

I stopped having sex, smoking, and getting drunk because it led me to destruction, pain, hurt, insecurities, and to becoming the person I didn't want to be. It led me to places I didn't ever want to go back to and places I would have never thought I would end up in.

Following Jesus and cutting these things out of my life was a difficult process, but I choose Jesus rather than a short-term fulfillment (Genesis 25:19-34). I stopped having sex because I want to have the most pleasure in marriage and in the right context. I stopped having sex because I love Jesus and trust him to lead me on a path of righteousness. I want my future spouse (God-willing) to feel special and loved because I chose purity.

It took a lot of work to stop those habits from happening again, as well as a lot of discipline in the process. Hebrews 12:11 reminds us, "No discipline seems pleasant at the time, but painful. Later on, however, it produces a harvest of righteousness and peace for those who have been trained by it."

When we follow God's design for our sexuality, we avoid a lot of pain, woundedness, and grieving. God designed sexuality so that we can experience intimacy, joy, and pleasure. Following his design allows us to do just that.

TORI'S STORY

One definition of *pure* is "free of any contamination." Before following Jesus, my life was the furthest thing from pure. It was cluttered with contamination of sexual sin, drug use, impure thoughts, jealousy, insecurity, and the list goes on. This left me empty, dissatisfied, and in a very dark place. I thought that there had to be more to this life. When someone introduced me to Jesus and the message of the gospel, my life was forever changed. I started following Jesus because there was no other option for me.

As I began to grow in intimacy with God, my mind began to be renewed, I was redeemed because of what Jesus did for me on the cross. The contamination of my sin was paid for. Having a pure heart paralleled my submission and commitment to the Lord. Now, because of this, I know God and how his hands are evident in every situation.

At times, when I start to fall into the cycle of doubt and ask myself why I began following Jesus in the first place, I remind myself of *all* that he saved me from. He saved me from depression, anxiety, and the consequences of my sin. On top of that, he gave me an abundant life. I follow Jesus because this world has nothing to compare to Jesus Christ and all that he offers to us.

Matthew 5:8 says, "Blessed are the pure in heart, for they will see God."

Romans 12:2 instructs us, "Do not conform to the pattern of this world, but be transformed by the renewing of your mind. Then you will be able to test and approve what God's will is—his good, pleasing and perfect will."

Learn more about the woman caught in adultery and how Jesus displays his deep love for her (John 8).

——— REFLECTION QUESTIONS ———

1. Why does God say sex outside of marriage isn't wise?

2. Why do you keep yourself pure?

3. Why is it important to not get drunk?

4. Why do you get high, drink, or have sex?

5. Why is it critical to obey Jesus in these worldly desires?

6. Why is it so hard to repent from sin and choose Jesus instead?

7. What lies am I believing around sex?

CHAPTER 12

SURRENDERING CONTROL

Why Should God Handle Your Finances?

This new generation has become obsessed with coffee shops. I love when I step through the doors of a modern coffee shop with dimmed lights; it brings me a sense of peace and comfort.

Since I seem to always be in a coffee shop, I have developed an addiction to caffeine. Unfortunately, having both a coffee addiction *and* a sweet tooth requires a lot of money.

I found this out the hard way.

For a long time, every morning I would hand the lady at the front counter my debit card like it was a piece of paper. I had no idea what was in my bank account and sometimes held my breath, hoping my payment would go through. In other words, I knew nothing about budgeting, nothing about saving money, and nothing about finances.

Today, I mentor girls about finances.

Here's my point: there is hope and redemption. It's not too late. You can start living differently—and wiser—today. No matter what shopping or coffee addiction you may have, God can help you get on track financially.

Why should you allow God to handle your finances? Here are five reasons:

BECAUSE IT'S LESS STRESSFUL!

The middle of my junior year of college, I had a crisis. I realized that once I graduated, I was going to have to pay off some debt. I was in complete panic mode because I wasn't taught anything about money growing up. I knew I had to push myself to learn the hows and whys behind paying off debt.

I started challenging things. I went to a Dave Ramsey class that taught me one way to pay off debt. Without knowing anything about budgeting, I became obsessed with this new approach. (I might have even gone a little overboard!)

I give a major shout-out to Dave Ramsey for helping me start a journey of peace and trust by giving God all of my control. Giving God the control of my finances offered me the peace and freedom to live with a lot less stress when it came to money.

NOT UNDERSTANDING MONEY LEADS TO MISTAKES AND EMBARRASSMENT

Being elected as the social chairwoman in my sorority brought me some major life lessons. I had to plan for the spring formal with a budget. Keep in mind, I had no idea how to budget money or the value of a dollar. My job roles were hiring a caterer, a bartender, a DJ, and security, securing a venue, ordering food, and renting a bus.

There were a whole lot of duties I had to manage, and I was not prepared for any of it. I didn't budget at all, and I was crowned the queen of go-with-the-flow. This led to destruction and eventually got me kicked out of my position.

It was a Thursday night, and everyone was all dressed up, heading to the venue. I was there before everyone arrived, and as soon as I stepped into the building, one security guard pulled me aside and proceeded to scream at me. Apparently, I didn't make it clear that there was going to be alcohol at the event with minors attending. She had to come on her day off to make sure they had enough people monitoring who was underage. Finding this out, I watched underage sorority girls haul their dates into the venue. With most of them wasted, I knew that I was going to be in deep doo-doo.

I didn't get a second security guard because it would cost a lot of money, and I knew I was already going to be over budget. I didn't think it was a huge deal because I was an innocent and privileged twenty-year-old who still had help from her parents with money. I soon got a slap in the face. The day after, I got a call from our sorority president, who preceded to tell me I went $2,000 over budget. Huge yikes. Were my goals completed of everyone having an amazing and fun formal? Oh, absolutely.

Did I have the wrong goals and get kicked out of my position because I was unprepared? You bet I did.

That huge mistake brought me regret and cost me my resignation from the position. However, it gave me a life lesson of how to manage my money. My goal is to remind you readers in this chapter to not make the same mistake I did and encourage you to ask yourself the whys when handling money.

Psalms and Proverbs have wisdom to share about finances: Psalm 37:21 says, "The wicked borrow and do not repay, but the righteous give generously." Proverbs 21:5 reminds us that "the plans of the diligent lead to profit, as surely as haste leads to poverty."

GOD PROVIDES

After I began to learn about budgets and money and started paying down my debt, I experienced some tight times. But God was faithful, and often he provided exactly what I needed when I needed it.

From a Door Dash customer who paid an extra-large tip, to friends who spontaneously handed me cash without knowing that I had less than ten dollars in my bank account at the time, I have seen God repeatedly honor my efforts to stay out of debt.

And it happened. I have spent the past couple of years determined to pay off all my debt in a reasonable time, and I accomplished it. God provides for me, but I have to do my part too. Sometimes it means eating simple food at home rather than eating out. It means not letting my obsessions with coffee and chocolate break the bank.

When we stop letting our fleshly love of spending create debt that puts us in bondage, we experience a sense of freedom that makes the sacrifices along the way seem small indeed.

BALANCE IS A GOOD THING

Balance is good. Out-of-control spending and debt makes life miserable. But it's also possible to be out of balance in the other direction. Believe it or not, it's possible to turn saving money and being frugal into idols. I know, because it happened to me.

Looking back, I originally decided to get out of debt because I had a fear of becoming like most Americans, who are drowning in debt. Every time I got a paycheck, I used most of it to pay off debt and ignored my basic needs. I was living off eggs and cereal because I refused to touch my savings. I wasn't trusting God at all. I wasn't using wisdom. I was trying to do everything on my own and had turned saving money into an idol.

I certainly didn't have any peace when my head hit the pillow at night.

Being in the right mindset when paying off debt is critical. As my income began to pick up, I didn't know when to say no. I ended up going down a rabbit hole of saying yes. I kept saying yes to things that would allow me to make money; in my head,

I just wanted to get rid of my debt no matter what. I worked fifty-five hours a week at three different jobs. I spread myself too thin and could barely walk because I was so exhausted.

I think paying off debt is a good thing, but it can easily become a bad thing when you allow your mental and physical health to go downhill. I think it's a good thing to give yourself some grace and say no to choices that ultimately drain you so that you can pick yourself up and have room for Jesus. Jesus is more important than paying off my debt. Jesus is more important than commitments. It's okay to reevaluate your priorities to make Jesus your first and foremost priority and commitment.

This life is about Jesus and others. Life is hard. I have watched close people in my life get drowned by their debt and overwhelmed by how much has been held over their head. I don't know what I would do in that situation. I think I would feel like I was drowning too. However, God can bring you out of debt no matter how much you feel like you are drowning in it.

Wherever we are in the process, developing the right heart and mindset toward money is a journey. The good news is that Jesus is next to us. He is sitting right next to us, holding our hand and feeling all our pain. He wants to lift us up and save us.

GOD IS PLEASED WHEN WE TITHE

At one point in my journey, I knew I wanted to give to God a tithe—ten percent—of my paycheck. The Bible encourages us to do this. Not because our salvation depends on it, but because God wants to release our anxieties and control by inviting us to open our hands.

God wants to release our anxieties and control by inviting us to open our hands.

When I first started tithing to my church, it was like someone gut-punched me in the throat. Not to be graphic or anything; that's just generally how I felt. Surrendering control freaking hurts. Letting go of money, pride, and security hurts. When you think that you have something that brings you security and comfort other than God, it is extremely hard to release.

But when I did, I felt an immediate release of anxiety and boost in my feelings of security and trust. It was an act of giving it to God and allowing him to take the reins of my situation and become number one in all areas.

Living in America, I seem to forget about how wealthy I am. Having a car in this country makes me privileged and in the top 5 to 8 percent of richest people on earth. Even having a fridge and a bed allows me to be privileged and blessed. We tend to become distracted with wanting more and more that we forget about how much we have right in front of us.

Tithing brought me contentment. I choose to tithe because it releases the fake sense of security and control I get from idolizing money; it also adjusts my priorities to trust God deeper.

SHELBY'S STORY

"If you will live like no one else now, then later you can live and give like no one else!" This is a quote I heard in high school while taking a financial course by Dave Ramsey. At the time, I was thinking, *What? That seems completely impossible!* And to be honest, I still feel that way sometimes, even after becoming debt-free!

I get asked a lot, "How did you do it?"

For me, there were just a few key things that helped me.

1. Listen to Dave Ramsey, and follow his debt snowball theory.

2. Give up small pleasures. You don't have to give up all of them, but find something in your budget that *can* go (or at least be enjoyed less often). For me, this was coffee. I love Starbucks, and when I added up how much I was spending there every month, I was shocked. I made the choice to buy a jug of iced coffee from the store, along with my favorite creamer, and that became my daily coffee. I still chose one day a week to treat myself, but I saved so much by making this small change.

3. When I get a tax return, I pay a large chunk toward my debt instead of having a shopping spree.

I wish I could say that the reason I became debt-free was to glorify God. However, if I'm being honest, I did it because

I knew that in our society, being financially fit is something everyone applauds. But even more important, removing my debt presented a beautiful opportunity to bring Jesus into my daily life choices. Every purchase I made or wanted to make was viewed through his lens. Knowing Jesus was concerned over how I managed money made me feel more accountable, and I also felt cared for.

Why do I follow Jesus? Because I have never known a love so true. A love that is sincerely unconditional. By following Jesus and having a relationship with him, I hope to share that kind of love with others. To love more and more like him as the days of my life go by. I know that by being debt-free, I have more freedom to give financially to local organizations, to my church, and to worldwide missions that share the love and hope found in Jesus.

Read more about what the bible says about money and what we should be doing to steward it well. Mark 10:17-30, Psalm 50:10, Proverbs 22:7, 1 Timothy 6:6, Matthew 6:19-21 Acts 20:35, 2 Corinthians 9:6, Hebrews 13:5, Proverbs 13:27

──────── REFLECTION QUESTIONS ────────

1. Why do I honor God with my money?

2. What does the Bible say about debt, and why should I listen?

3. What does it mean to tithe, and why should I participate?

4. Why am I hoarding my money and not paying down debt or giving it to the local church?

5. Have I given the authority of finances over to God? Am I serving God or money?

CHAPTER 13

ALL ABOUT JESUS

Why Follow the Basics?

When I started pursuing Jesus, I was doing it the way my campus ministry did it. I learned so much about how to follow Jesus, but my motives were wrong. I started idolizing the ministry rather than following Jesus in my own way. I started to fit God inside of a box. I got so obsessed with the idea of doing things *for* God that I completely forgot to live a life *with* God.

The moment when I started actually following him on my own was when I paused and took a step back. I found myself going to a church's college night at a local coffee shop and fell in love with the way these people followed Jesus. They were real and brutally honest about where they were at with God.

I had never experienced that before. One of the speakers that night spoke about how he opens his Bible in the middle of the day because he feels closest to God at 1:00 p.m. I thought this idea was taboo because I was always taught to have quiet time with God when I woke up in the morning.

I realized that there are so many different ways you can be pursuing Jesus. Where do you feel God's presence the most? In your room, at a coffee shop, outside in nature, with a friend? Getting in a habit of going to one of those places every day may change your entire day, week, month, or year.

For me, I love going to coffee shops or simply opening my window with a cup of coffee and playing my favorite Spotify playlists.

The point is, go back to the gospel when you are feeling lost. Go back to your testimony. Get obsessed with what Jesus has done for you. As my friend Ben says, "Get wrecked by the gospel."

Go back to the gospel when you are feeling lost.

Reminding yourself of God's character is critical. The truths of God and who he is are constantly at war with the devil's voice and lies. God loves us so much that he sent his one and only Son, Jesus, on the cross for our sins so that we can have a relationship with him. Satan twists Scripture, but God is a good God. Reminding yourself of God's character can completely change the trajectory of your life. It's not about the fruit; it's about the source. It's all about Jesus.

When I learned that following Jesus is about having a relationship with him and not a religion, my life changed. It's not about following tradition; it's about finding Jesus. I got caught in the traditions of Christianity rather than falling in love with Jesus. Some people see Jesus clearer in traditional ways of Christianity, but that is definitely not me.

Every person who walks with Jesus is unique. My relationship with Jesus is different than yours. These are questions and topics to wrestle with God on your own. But here are the basics I hold onto that help me cling onto Jesus.

FELLOWSHIP: HANGING OUT WITH OTHER BELIEVERS CHANGES EVERYTHING

One of the basics described in the Bible is *fellowship*.

Having godly, Christian friends has been the most beneficial and amazing thing I have experienced. I prayed for wholesome and godly friends my freshman year of college, and boy did God exceed my expectations by a long shot. He blessed me with friends who would speak life into me, who would go on long car drives and talk about how Jesus was working in our lives. God has exceeded my expectations, and I am extremely blessed to still have relationships with these girls.

There was one night I had just walked out of a talk that had convicted me. It was getting really deep, and I wasn't sure how I was able to ever tell my best friends my deepest secret that I resonated with after that talk. I have never told anyone that I struggled with masturbation. I thought I was the only girl who had ever struggled with this. When I opened up to a small group of close friends, I came to find out that all of those friends struggled with the exact same thing. I was shocked. I was relieved. I was encouraged. I was strengthened.

This is *why* opening up to trusted and godly friends is worth it.

Fellowship is worth it. Getting pushed beyond my abilities because of godly friends and being inspired by their love for Jesus has inspired me to love Jesus deeper.

Secrets pull us down.

Because of the secret I had kept for so long, I didn't think that God could love me or that I was capable of forgiving myself and allowing him to love me.

Sis, let God love you. Let God enter your life and love you in those dark places, those dark wounds. He is here for you. He knows and loves your heart, and he wants to align your heart to his will. You don't need to do anything but accept the grace and forgiveness he offers.

When I was a senior in college, I was surrounded by some amazing sisters in Christ through a small group called "Sisterhood." These girls were meant to be placed in my life for a season. These girls taught me what it was like to fully embrace the love of Jesus by being real and embracing our imperfections and brokenness. This group was filled with strong women who have been through some crap. Yet they each had incredible radiance shining from them.

The last time we met, we gave each other blessings of words of encouragement. I have never done this before, but when I wrote each girl's blessing, I felt the Holy Spirit. Later, as we read our blessings to each other, it was absolutely remarkable how much our messages aligned; the Holy Spirit had spoken through each of us. We spoke to each other's souls, spoke into places for which we wouldn't have had words without inviting the Holy Spirit into the process. When we spoke our blessings over each other, it was remarkable.

Freshman Lindsea was lost. I didn't have many Christian friends to pick me back up and was surrounded by friends who dragged me down. "Friends" who would drag me to parties, get me drunk, and pass me something to smoke. This brought me to a dark place.

So instead, I decided to pray. Within a year, I had gained an entire community of believers. God answered my prayers but blew me away in the process because I gained an amazing, godly friend group.

I sit with all of you girls reading this, feeling like you are alone. I sit with all of you girls reading this, feeling like you don't want to ever leave your group of non-Christian friends. I sit with all of you girls reading this who think you aren't good enough for godly friends.

Take a chance. Ask God to bring you into a community of godly friends. Ask him to bring you into a place of uplifting fellowship. Ask him and see what happens next.

MERCY AND GRACE: THEY ARE FOUNDATIONAL TO HOW GOD RELATES TO YOU

I heard this analogy from a mentor when I was in college, and it helped me grasp the difference between mercy and grace.

Let's say you're driving on the highway going 150 miles per hour in a 75-mile-per-hour zone, and a cop spots you on the highway and pulls you over. You are sitting in the car, freaking out, thinking you are going to get arrested for reckless driving because you were exceeding the speed limit and deserve to have your license taken away.

The cop comes to your window. But instead of giving you the punishment that you deserve, he decides to let you off with a warning. That's mercy.

But wait! Before he leaves, he gifts you three hundred-dollar bills. He does this knowing that you will indeed speed again. *That's* grace.

I am thankful for a merciful God who doesn't give me the punishments I deserve; instead, he shows me grace by saving me and giving me more blessings than I can even wrap my brain around.

Applying this "foundational mindset" means accepting mercy. It means accepting grace.

Stop running from God. Pull your car over and accept those hundred-dollar bills.

Praise God. Praise him. It's never too late to repent and accept these gifts from him. His way is better than yours. It may take courage to pull your runaway car to the side of the road and see what he has for you, but guess what? He is waiting, and he is patient. He is chasing after us. He doesn't want traffic fines and jail time for us; he offers forgiveness, freedom, and blessings.

TRUTH: GOD'S TRUTH WILL CHANGE YOUR PERSPECTIVE—AND YOUR LIFE

Over the years, my eyesight has dramatically decreased. I wouldn't necessarily say that I am blind, but I also wouldn't say that I can see completely clear. When I first got glasses, I was driving on the road to school, and I was amazed about how clear the traffic light looked. I was so shocked because I didn't think that it was supposed to look that clear. I thought my vision was the best it could get until I put those glasses on.

If we have been living one way for all our life, we can get the feeling that our situation is normal. We think it doesn't get any better than how we view it. Once we admit that we need glasses, we see things a whole lot better and a whole lot clearer.

Having a relationship with Jesus and discovering the truths revealed in his Word allows our vision to become clearer.

I thought that it was normal to have sex in high school and get drunk every weekend. Come to find out, the way I was living was blurry and foggy until I put the glasses of truth on. Putting on a new prescription may hurt sometimes, but I assure you that doing so brings more clarity. My life has never been better. I have never felt this much joy and life by just seeing clearly.

It all came from reading God's word. It came from God softening my heart over the years to the truth and wisdom of his principles. Just like I had to choose to wear glasses in order to see clearer, I had to choose to apply God's truth by changing old patterns in my life. I had to believe what I read in the Bible and pay attention when my mentors and friends told me that how I'd been living wasn't part of God's plan for me.

Sin separates us from God. That is why it is important to follow the truth of the word. When I chose to not obey God's truth, it led to destruction.

The other week, I had something in my eye for three days. I tried everything to get it out, but I couldn't see what was in it. It took over my entire body at one point. I had to lay down, turn the lights off, and cry out to the Lord because I was in so much pain because of a small speck in my eye.

It made me realize that this little tiny thing that was in my eye was an example of sin. Sin can overcome your whole body; one lie or one sin can ruin everything. It starts with poor vision, then leaves you paralyzed and crying out in the darkness.

The good news is that wherever you are, God has the power to take your sin completely away. He provides the truth we need to heal our vision so we can get back up and turn the lights on.

Romans 2:8 says, "But for those who are self-seeking and who reject the truth and follow evil, there will be wrath and anger."

A part of truth is hope. Jesus provides us hope because he conquered death, which allowed us to have a loving relationship with him. Also, he will one day return to bring heaven back to this broken world. Heaven isn't the end for us. Life after heaven is our hope because we will be living in this world with new bodies and Jesus will make us new. He saved us. That's hope.

When we start becoming numb with sin and following our feelings instead of God's truth, we are on a dangerous path. When we stop looking at the truth, it can cause more pain than God has intended for us. It can even hurt God because of how much he deeply cares for us. The truth is a good thing, even if our feelings tell us the lies make us feel better.

My dad and I had an off-and-on again relationship in high school. Because of my dad's pain, he chose lies over truth, thinking it would help but; in the end, it only hurt everyone around him. He lied to try to make people feel better about certain situations. But it only resulted in broken and strained relationships.

Throughout high school, I didn't know the difference between my dad's lies and his truths. These experiences affected my relationship with God. When I started walking in a relationship with him, it was hard to believe the truth of what God said and that it was good.

Our fathers, mothers, grandmas, and grandpas are broken and are sinners. It isn't their fault. When your fatherly or motherly figure hasn't modeled the character of God, it can lead our truths to be lies—or make it hard to believe the truth.

The good thing about Jesus is that we can hold onto the

truth written in the Bible. We can open Scripture and have that right in front of us. It starts by trusting what the Bible has to say and when you feel differently you still have truth you trust.

We can trust those words because God fulfills his promises. It took me awhile to trust God with who he says he is, that being said, I encourage you to pray, dive in to scripture, read theology books or listen to Christian podcasts to learn more about who God is. We can't let the devil's lies get to us. When we continue to fall, we can continue to get up because we have the arms of Jesus to lift us to higher ground. The truth ultimately saves us.

When we skew the truth, then it gets messy. We can't walk straight when we are living in a lie; we may end up going in the wrong direction. We need the full truth of Jesus as our guiding compass. That starts with trusting the bible fully and not only picking verses out that make you feel good. Truth can hurt sometimes, however, it always leads to wisdom and life.

THE HOLY SPIRIT: HE IS REAL AND WILL COMFORT AND GUIDE YOU

Let God snuggle you with the Holy Spirit.

The Bible says that after Jesus ascended to heaven, God sent his Holy Spirit to comfort and guide us. The Holy Spirit is our Helper and guides us using the truth. "When the Advocate comes, whom I will send to you from the Father—the Spirit of truth who goes out from the Father—he will testify about me" (John 15:26).

Water comes in three different forms; ice, liquid and solid. We can trust that no matter what form, it is still water. Exactly how we can trust the holy trinity as the Father, Son and Holy Spirit. God is with us through the Holy Spirit every single day. How cool is that? When was the last time you simply paused and asked the Holy Spirit to guide your day? When was the last time you put your hands out in an act of surrender from your flesh and simply listened to the spirit?

Sometimes I will spend days on end just praying and asking God to change certain things about my life and other people's lives. I will pray out loud in the car, pray in my head, or pray until I fall asleep. God tells us to pray without ceasing, but he also wants us to pause and listen to what he has to say.

1 Thessalonians 5:16–18 says, "Rejoice always, pray continually, give thanks in all circumstances; for this is God's will for you in Christ Jesus."

Psalm 37:7 encourages us to "be still before the LORD and wait patiently for him; do not fret when people succeed in their ways, when they carry out their wicked schemes."

John 10:27 says, "My sheep listen to my voice; I know them, and they follow me." Sheep know how the Shepherd talks. This means we need to know the character of God in able to determine the voice we are following through the Holy Spirit. Jesus knows exactly what we need. He talks to us with words like they are prescriptions to our heart. He is loving and will never guide us to evil or contrary from his word.

When I wake up in the morning, I want to get my coffee, eat breakfast, and have some quiet time with God in peace and in silence. Typically, though, that doesn't happen, especially when I am at my mom's house. I try to go about my morning slowly, but my mom comes out of her room just talking to me about everything, including how her day was yesterday, what she is doing today, her thoughts on current events, questions about my plans, and so on.

This isn't a bad thing. In fact, it's sweet how she loves me enough to bring her thoughts and energy to me. Her heart is in the right place, and it brings me joy when she feels comfortable telling me about everything in her soul.

I can think of a time in my life when I did the exact same thing. My senior year of college I lived in a house called the Honeycomb with two sweet roommates. We all loved quiet mornings when we could tune out the world and listen to Jesus. But for some reason, every morning I turned into a chatterbox. Looking back, I realize I probably annoyed the crap out of them talking and talking about random things.

It got me thinking. How does God feel about me doing all the talking when we're together? We were created in God's image. Since we as man communicate with each other, it also means that God loves talking to us too. In fact, he wants to talk to us, comfort us and protect us. He loves listening, and he knows our hearts. He finds joy in hearing about our days, and thoughts, and feelings.

But sometimes God wants to talk back to us, and we haven't given him a chance. God wants to lead us with his Holy Spirit but we are sometimes too consumed by this world to be able to follow his voice.

What if we were to pause and sit in silence for two minutes out of each day? Or even sat and thanked and praised God for everything that he has done? What if God wanted to place a name on your heart to pray for them or tell you a provision that he has for you, but instead you were the one interrupting? What if God simply justs wants to be with you because he loves you?

When I developed a meeker attitude in my mornings at the Honeycomb, I found myself hearing God clearer. My days started off a lot better because I was able to have the God of the universe align my path straighter by a simple act of silence.

One morning, I had plans to spend the evening at a bar that had one-dollar mixed drinks. As I spent time listening, I felt an urging from the Holy Spirit to be the sober driver and not to drink that night. I knew it was from God because it aligned with Romans 13:13.

That night, as people asked why I wasn't drinking, I had the opportunity to share my faith with them. All because of a simple act of silence and obedience to the Holy Spirit. Choosing to listen to the nudge of the Holy Spirit gave me the opportunity to share my faith and tell others why I wasn't drinking. Although it's not what I wanted to do whatsoever, I knew remaining sober was the right thing to do because I knew God's character through his word, the Holy Bible. It ultimately glorified God and was life-giving to me.

I pursue Jesus and his Holy Spirit every day because the majority of the time my days lead to regret and destruction if I don't. We are nowhere near perfect, and that's exactly why surrendering our control daily and inviting the Holy Spirit into our choices and our days is so important.

SILENCE: GOD MEETS US THERE

When was the last time you were still and listened to God? When was the last time you sat down and tuned out the loudness of the world? When was the last time you put your phone down, turned the TV off, logged out of social media, and got away from the noise of family and friends? When was the last time you turned the music off and sat in silence? I hate sitting around and doing nothing. I will fill every minute of my day doing anything but sitting with my own thoughts. When I have free time, I choose to get on my phone and fill my brain with meaningless content. Sitting in silence is probably the hardest thing to do.

One wintery day after work, I decided to drive around this

beautiful reservoir in Fort Collins called Hoosetooth. It simply takes your breath away. As I was finally driving home, I looked to my right and saw a fox running in the middle of the frozen lake.

I pulled over as fast as I could because this never happens. Gazing at the fox, I was in complete silence. I looked at the beautiful sunset view with a fox running over the glazed frozen reservoir. As I went home, it dawned on me that the fox is a symbol for silence. God was trying to tell me something, but I wasn't comprehending it yet.

The following weekend, I went on a spontaneous road trip to New Mexico with my best friend. On the drive there, we prayed for God to reveal the desires of our hearts and for his perspective on our lives. The minute we drove into Santa Fe, a cop looked at us, gave us huge hand gestures, and yelled at us to slow down.

That moment stuck with us the rest of the trip. My friend and I are both busy people. We take in content consistently and fill up our schedules with coffee dates without having room to breathe. That weekend, in fact, was a bit like that too. We filled up our time constantly by seeing new views and eating new foods.

Before starting our long drive home, we stopped at my friend's favorite coffee shop. As we enjoyed each other's company and our hot matcha tea, I turned my head to my right, and there was a boy wearing a fox mask.

It wasn't until we were on the long drive back home, with

no service and silence, that we fully grasped what God was doing. God was reminding us to slow down and delight in him. Psalm 37:4 says, "Take delight in the LORD, and he will give you the desires of your heart." How cool is that? We had prayed for the Lord to show us the desires of our heart, and his message to us was to embrace silence and, in that silence, his very presence.

To top it all off, it wasn't long before we passed a massive fox billboard on the highway. Once again, I felt the nudge of the Holy Spirit confirming that we were to delight in him and to take time to be silent.

Being silent has completely changed the way I follow Jesus. I have realized the value of being *with* him and not doing things *for* Him.

The overwhelming joy I feel even in the midst of chaos is because I choose to *be* with God every day and not *do* things for him. Missing a quiet time with him doesn't change my day anymore, because I have learned that he is right next to me the entire day and that I can delight in him. I encourage you to set a timer and take two to five minutes to simply sit in silence and see what God does. Picture Jesus sitting next to you, hugging you or delighting in the things that you enjoy. I encourage you to take a 24-hour sabbath every week with your phone off and doing things you love. This is so you can unplug from the world and listen to Jesus.

SPIRITUAL WARFARE: WE HAVE AN ENEMY

Lust is fun. Drinking is fun. Sex is fun. Getting high is fun. Smoking a Juul is fun. Doing bad things is fun. (At least for a short time until the pain starts and destruction comes.) Let me be real with you for a second. Sometimes I just want to give up because I think that living in sin will be easier. Following Jesus is hard sometimes. But these feelings and thoughts are all lies and don't come from God.

That's what spiritual warfare does. The devil is working even when we don't realize it. He brings across our paths things we think look good and things we think will fulfill us. It's not until we fall flat on our faces that we realize we are back where we started and never wanted to end up again. John 10:9-10 says "I am the gate; whoever enters through me will be saved. They will come in and go out, and find pasture. The thief comes only to steal and kill and destroy; I have come that they may have life, and have it to full."

Sin is an endless cycle. You start drinking, end up doing something stupid that you regret, then you do it all again.

We don't do it because our memories are bad.

We actually have an enemy who seeks to tempt us and make us stumble at every turn. We have an enemy who HATES us. He wants us to die. 1 Peter 5:8 says "Be alert and of sober mind. Your enemy the devil prowls around like a roaring lion looking for someone to devour."

Getting serious when it comes to spiritual warfare is crucial. I run away as fast as I can from Ouija boards, spiritual card games, crystals, manifesting spirits, drugs, and a lot more "cultural" games because that brings dark forces into the world (Leviticus 19:31). But we don't only battle obvious symbols of the occult. Sometimes we have to battle our own thoughts. For example, I run as fast as I can when a thought pops in my head that says, "I want to sleep with that guy" or "I want to smoke that Juul."

The Bible tells us to take every thought captive. "We demolish arguments and every pretension that sets itself up against the knowledge of God, and we take captive every thought to make it obedient to Christ" (2 Corinthians 10:5). That means being intentional about which thoughts you dwell on and which you reject.

I want to get closer to God, not farther away from Him. The good news is that when you accept Jesus in your heart, these forces can't touch you, but they can tempt you. Accepting Jesus means you belong to him, and no one—not even the enemy of our souls—can change that. Jesus fights for us even when we can't see or feel it. We have a good, good God. He wants to protect us from these demonic forces.

REPENT: JESUS DIED FOR ALL YOUR PAST SINS—AND YOUR FUTURE SINS TOO

I love taking spontaneous trips. I don't know if it's because I like adventure or because I enjoy running away from my problems.

A group of my friends and I booked a trip to San Diego last minute to stay with some of our friends. I had different expectations of this trip than what it turned out to be. All six of us who went on this trip were in the middle of facing challenges, big and small. In other words, we each brought mental baggage and personal pain with us. During the trip, we each fell into sin trying to medicate that pain and find relief with something other than Jesus.

Drinking, smoking, kissing . . . Whatever we use to self-medicate and fill ourselves with will never lead to satisfaction. Jesus is our satisfaction.

One thing that I learned from that long weekend trip was that no matter how much we continue to fall in the same sin patterns and continue to mess up, we can repent and receive Jesus' forgiveness right on the spot.

It's easy to fall into the trap of thinking, *Well, sure. Jesus forgave my sins the first time I asked him. But how can I talk to him about this new failure? After I have a relationship with him, I'm not supposed to sin again, right?*

After we have a relationship with Jesus, we try to avoid sin because of the pain it causes him, us and people around us. We reject lifestyles of sin. We try every day to make choices that honor God and bring blessing to ourselves and those around us.

But sometimes we fail.

Repent, accept his forgiveness, and move on.

When we hold onto guilt for our mistakes, it gives our enemy a foothold into our minds. It gives him the chance to leverage that guilt into more sin and more separation from God.

HANG OUT WITH UNBELIEVERS: JESUS DID, SO WHY AREN'T YOU?

The six feet apart rule and social distancing established from COVID-19, made me realize something. Is this how the marginalized feel when we treat them with disrespect? As soon as someone interacts with someone that has COVID-19, people run away from them. Jesus cared for these people (Mark 2:13-17). He cared for the people that were the outcasts, the homeless, the murderers. If Jesus did this, what makes us feel entitled to not love these people?

In Mark 2:13-17, Jesus heals a man with Leprosy. This man was shunned, untouched, and judged every single day. But yet, Jesus loved him exactly where he was at. He knew him. He saw him. He loved him and cared for him, even though the crowd did otherwise.

After church, I decided to go on a drive and blast my music. I drove past a cute mountain brunch spot that happened to be on the road I was driving on. I ended up pulling in and parking. They had coffee-to-go, and I knew that it was calling my name. As I walked up to the counter and ordered a cup of coffee, I had a sense this server was going to give me this coffee for free.

He came back, and sure enough, he said, "on the house today."

I felt like God whispered to me, "I got you coffee today because I love you."

I smiled. The sweet God of the universe loves me.

After my drive, I was driving back home and stopped for gas. As it was below freezing, I recognized the homeless woman on the side of the road. I thought she would enjoy a warm cup of coffee. I went to the gas station and purchased a $1.25 cup of joe.

I walked up to sweet Marina and gave her a cup of coffee. I learned about her story and spoke to her about her morning. I found out that sweet Marina just got baptized! Praise Jesus!

Jesus gave me the perfect image of what it means to pour his love out on others. As we get poured into by the love of God, we can pour out his love to others. However, we can't love on our strength.

Matthew 22:27 says, "Jesus replied: "Love the Lord your God with all your heart and with all your soul and with all your mind. This is the first and greatest commandment. And the second is like it: "Love your neighbor as yourself.""

Remembering the basics can be hard. Remind yourself on your own time with you and your own personal relationship with God.

Hang out with other believers. Accept mercy and grace. Understand and believe God's truths. Follow the nudgings of the Holy Spirit. Be silent and listen. Battle against the enemy. Accept forgiveness every day. Love others as Jesus loves you.

MADISON'S STORY

I grew up as a Christmas and Easter Christian who only went to church because I was told it's what I had to do. My sister became friends with a family that was involved in a local church. She gave her life to God, and everything changed for her.

We had grown up in a dysfunctional household and ended up leaning on each other during the times of dealing with our parents. Because of this, my sister was like a second mom to me. I was going to youth group and church regularly because she asked me to go. Whenever I went to youth group, I always felt like there was a moment I was missing out on. My sister had a moment, and her entire life was instantly changed. However, that wasn't working for me. I tried and tried. It felt like faith was not for me. My faith was entirely dependent on my sister. Soon, my sister graduated high school and moved away. When I started going to church alone, the pastor had just been arrested for sexual assault.

Despite some people's best efforts, the church was broken and unhealthy. Years later, the dysfunction in my church was growing in all different directions. My feelings became deeply hurt by the things that were happening. As a result, I left in the middle of a service and never went back. Slowly, I abandoned Jesus. I started to not recognize myself. I lived out of a desire to get other people's approval. I was a people pleaser.

As college started, I was finally out of an unhealthy environment and thought I would flourish! But I did not seem to make friends as fast as everyone else. I was not as smart or as fun as the people around me. Feelings as though I had no friends and no support system weighed heavily on me.

That weight continued and continued until I was suffocating. I fought to find any reason to be alive. My anxiety was horrible, and my self-worth was in the gutter. I couldn't do this life with my own strength. So I ended up letting go of my control and trusting in God's strength, as it says in Philippians 4:13.

Then things started changing.

Slowly, I made friends through a campus ministry and felt fully loved and supported by them. I also got connected with a lovely, healthy church. I realized that God was directing my path (Psalm 23:3). There was not a huge miracle that made my life instantly change, like my sisters. It was the small, everyday miracles that made me believe and trust in God. After I trusted God, I felt peace in hard circumstances and throughout his beauty in nature. Because of this, I knew I didn't want to continue to live the life I was living before God entered it. There was no joy in the route I was going down, and I needed something else.

Over time, I began to slowly read my Bible, pray more, and read Christian novels. I made the decision to follow God every single day. I began to realize that although I felt like Jesus was far from me, he had always been right next to me (Deuteronomy 31:8). Why do I follow Jesus? Because if he is not real then, I'm wasting my life here on earth. But if he is real, then that is everything.

Remind yourself why you follow the basics through scripture. Romans 12:2, Ephesians 6:10-11, 2 Corinthians 10:4-5, James 1:26, 1 Thessalonians 5:11, Hebrews 10:25, Hebrews 4:16, Matthew 9:13

——— REFLECTION QUESTIONS ———

1. Why should you remind yourself of the basics of God's love and what he offers each of us?

2. Why is it important to become grounded in truth, grace, and fellowship?

3. How can fellowship bring me closer to God?

4. Why do I run away from grace?

5. Why is it important to listen to the Holy Spirit and be aware of spiritual warfare?

6. Why do I run away from silence?

7. Why is a Sabbath day important?

CHAPTER 14

LIFE CHANGES
Why Obey?

I was in multiple toxic relationships in high school and in the beginning of college. I was still in a dark place even though I believed in God. I had shallow quiet times in the morning and was occasionally talking to God. But I was getting drunk, having sex, and not being the person I wanted to be. I loved the attention that boys gave me. I was manipulating others, and I let guilt and shame take over my life. I was convinced that God couldn't love or want someone like me.

Whatever the details, here's what it boiled down to: I wasn't able to fully live in God's freedom because I was a slave to my sin. I was a slave to my flesh. I was latching onto anything other than him, and it always brought me hurt and destruction. It took me forever to remember why being obedient to God was the right way. Our flesh may tell us one thing about feelings, but God directs us with his truth.

One ordinary day, I made a decision that changed everything.

I decided to obey God by listening to his truths and following his commandments. It was in that moment that my life changed. I began to experience abundance and peace.

I continue to take steps toward Jesus through my obedience to him and by following his will. I can say my commitment to follow God is the best decision I have ever made in my life; it's the best decision you can make too. But you have to *remember why* you are obeying God and *remember why* his way is the best way.

OBEYING GOD WILL BRING YOU PEACE AND HOPE

Following God's instruction will change your life. Being obedient will bring you peace, give you hope, and bring you a life that you never thought you would have.

I remember when I'd finally had enough of my own rebellious choices. I woke up one morning after a night of getting the most drunk I'd ever been. I didn't remember a thing from the night before. I certainly didn't remember calling my ex-boyfriend to come pick me up because I was too hammered to drive—or the fact that I was flirting with other guys when he arrived.

The mess that I created and the hurt that I caused impacted a lot of people.

I was devastated.

I didn't want to hurt anyone else ever again. I never wanted to wake up, hungover, finding out I hurt someone I cared about. For the first time, I saw how weak I was and how incapable I was of doing anything without the Lord.

That was the start of my journey in being obedient to God. God brings light, healing, peace, and allows our wounds to be cleaned and healed correctly. We aren't meant to clean up our sin on our own. In fact, it is impossible. That's exactly why Jesus died on that cross.

I finally listened to God and to what he was telling me to do: let go of control.

And as I did, God began transforming my life into something that wasn't filled with shame and guilt; instead, I became filled with his divine freedom and abundance.

Following God's design and instructions makes me strong, fulfilled, joyful, and abundant. He brings me love so I can love others deeply. He saved me from hell and loves me just as I am, a sinner.

You can't do this life on your own. You are weak and God is strong. He makes us strong! We need to humble ourselves and listen to God's instructions and promptings. He will direct our life and bring us freedom, out of our free will. This moment is different for everyone, and God is patient with us.

God is patient with us.

OBEDIENCE—EVEN WHEN IT'S HARD—BRINGS BLESSINGS

I wanted to move to Austin, Texas, so badly after college. I wanted to run away and start over and make new friends and find a new church. But when I humbly asked God what I should do, I stumbled upon a verse that said "wait." Although I was frustrated with him and mad at the idea of staying put, I decided to listen to him because I believe his way is the best way.

I stayed put.

Then COVID-19 happened, and suddenly it made sense why God had told me to wait. I got to save money, build a deeper connection with my family, get closer to my friends, and find healing.

This was all because I obeyed God even when I didn't like what he was telling me to do.

Being obedient to God allowed my life to align with his desire to bless and protect me. When you're a kid and you don't know any better, your parents are the ones who grab you from running into an open street, limit your bank account so you don't overspend, and make you eat veggies so you don't become unhealthy. Our parents merely want the best for us so we don't get hurt or have regrets or kill ourselves by running into an open, traffic-heavy street.

Isn't that what God is trying to do with us?

It's not like he wants to hurt us or doesn't want us to have fun with life. In fact, he wants the opposite. He wants us to have a fulfilling life that brings us endless love and peace rather than one that sends us reeling down a road of destruction.

We are not alone in this. God is here to help us as we seek to obey him.

The first semester of my senior year, I felt God directing me, through Scripture, to break up with my ex-boyfriend. Our lives weren't aligning fully with the truth of what the Bible said. However, it didn't make sense at all, according to my feelings. We had tried to put God in the center of our relationship, so why should I break up with him? I began to question God.

At the same time, I knew there were some things in our relationship that weren't honoring to God. We both were not equally yoked because we were in two different stages in life—both with God and in our desires for the future. It took me a while to obey God in his truth to break up with him, but I eventually did it.

As a result, we have both experienced a great renewal and new chapter in our love for Jesus. We are submitted to God's word like never before. God had a plan and knew we would glorify him more out of the relationship than in it.

Continuing to be obedient to the Lord is hard, but it's worth it.

The other day, I was on a run and got this image of what our lives can begin to look like when we simply obey Jesus: things start falling into place; things start making sense. It's beautiful!

But to get to that point there is a lot of trust involved. It took me a long time to get to the point where I am in trusting God today. Much like a bike with training wheels, it takes practice to trust that you can take those training wheels off. Hebrews 12:11 says, "No discipline seems pleasant at the time, but painful. Later on, however, it produces a harvest of righteousness and peace for those trained by it."

WHEN WE OBEY GOD, WE'RE NOT AS LIKELY TO HURT THE PEOPLE WE LOVE

I grew up in a household that was a bit manipulative and filled with a lot of lies. There are some things I'll never know were true.

My parents got a divorce when I was in high school. My mom tells me that they got a divorce because my dad cheated on her. But my dad tells me that he would never cheat on her. So, who do I trust? Who am I supposed to believe?

I remember sitting on our cozy basement couch with my siblings sitting next to me when we learned that our family was falling apart. Our dad was pacing back and forth in front of us, about to tell us something he never thought he would have too.

My head began to ring and spin as he finally said the words, "Your mom and I are getting a divorce." I jumped off the couch, sprinted upstairs, grabbed the keys to my Toyota Camry, and ran out the door as fast as I could. My sister chased after me, calling my name. But I barely heard her. I could think of only one thing: the dissolution of our family.

I drove as fast as I could to the only secluded place I could think of: the back of a parking lot at a family sports center. I was having an anxiety attack; everything in my body felt like it was shutting down. I was blasting music in my car and wanted to run away and drown out the world around me forever. I didn't want to think about anything else. My phone got blown up by my high school boyfriend and by my sister. Notification after notification flashed on my phone screen.

I couldn't think straight. Eventually, I texted back that I wasn't doing okay, and they rushed to my side. That was one of the darkest spots mentally I have ever been in.

Because of the betrayal I felt, it took me a long time to begin to trust Jesus and his promises. It is a process. I took baby steps. My eyes would open a little bit more as I would release my chains. As I continued to surrender small areas of my life to Jesus, the more I saw him working. He never *wasn't* working in my life, but now I am actually able to see it and be aware of it.

The mistakes of my parents hurt me. My mistakes hurt others.

Until we're in heaven, we will continue to make choices that hurt the people we love, even if we don't intent too. When we seek to obey God and make choices that are in sync with his will for us and his design for us, the less carnage we will create in the lives of those around us.

The moment we choose to obey, God overflows us with his love and comfort. He wants to remind us that he loves us. He loves us. Me. You, reading this book. No matter what we have done, God runs after us and invites us to experience his love and comfort. God's love language is obedience.

On top of that, he overwhelms us with blessings. We don't deserve these blessings, but he gives them to us because he loves us. However, don't fall in the trap of feeling like you deserve these blessings (John 8:1-11).

I encourage you to continue to receive his goodness and mercy and come to him. His mercies are new every morning (Lamentations 3:22-23).

OBEYING GOD HALFWAY LEAVES US UNFULFILLED

I refused to be completely obedient to the Lord for about a year when I had surrendered my life to him. I kept getting caught up in lust (even though I wasn't having sex), found myself in the bar scene (even though I wasn't getting drunk), and I found myself completely empty and unfulfilled. I would come home every night or wake up in the morning and be filled with utter darkness and sadness.

My world felt broken; things didn't feel right.

I look back now and recognize that I had I placed myself in temptation and grey areas that were leading me toward the wrong path. As soon as I repented and surrounded myself with the right people and right places, my world shifted. I felt free because I was obedient and surrendered it all to Jesus.

1 John 2:17 says, "The world and its desires pass away, but whoever *does* the will of God lives forever" (emphasis added).

Choosing to continue to be obedient to Jesus, I get to see that God is flooding me with blessings upon blessings that I do not deserve whatsoever. Being obedient and letting God do his work over my life has brought me an extensive amount of healing. But I had to release my pride and allow God to humble me so that he could change my motives and soften my heart.

OBEYING GOD CAN BROADEN OUR WORLD AND OUR IMPACT

A sorority sister and I had coffee one morning. She told me a story that stuck with me. She had recently gone on a trip with YWAM (Youth With A Mission) to Australia. Before making that decision, however, she was scared to make a change and move away from her family and friends. She describes herself as a homebody who loves comfort! But she took a leap of faith and didn't let being uncomfortable stop her from a life-changing experience.

She told me that she was shocked about how God used her in incredible ways and how many people God brought across her path. God brings us people to us wherever we go. How cool is that?

It got me thinking about how often I have let the comfortable "American dream" lifestyle overshadow my obedience in God. What if being uncomfortable allows us to grow and change in remarkable ways that we can't even fathom?

Being obedient is difficult. But I want to remind you that God is patient with you. He will continue to fight for you and be with you every step of the way. Lean in, listen, and be encouraged by him.

James 4:8 offers encouragement: "Come near to God and he will come near to you." The Lord is near right now, and it is never too late to begin to be obedient to him.

When I made the choice to stop obeying my fleshly wants and start obeying God, it didn't make my life suddenly easy. But it did allow me to **experience peace in the middle of chaos.** When my life feels like it is falling apart around me, I know I'm on the right path when it aligns with God's truth. And when things I plan get cancelled, peace floods me because I know that I'm in the center of God's will, and he has something better planned for me.

Right after an internship got cancelled, blessings flooded. Leadership opportunities, fellowship, spiritual growth programs, and options for jobs began to open up.

When you choose to be obedient, you see God's plans for your life in a new light.

Matthew 7:7 says, "Ask and it will be given to you; seek and you will find; knock and the door will be opened to you."

Don't believe me? Give it a try sometime. Or maybe take a step back and consider that God's ways are not our ways.

God wants our life to be fruitful and blessed.

What if you put your pride and stubbornness aside and let God do the work?

Matthew 23:12 offers encouragement: "For those who exalt themselves will be humbled, and those who humble themselves will be exalted." Being obedient can be beneficial in your life even when you think you can do it on your own or you feel like the world is against you.

What if you truly believed, as I do, that God wants you to be joyful? What if a step toward obedience allowed that to happen? What sacrifices do you need to make to get there? Being obedient all starts with recognizing you need a savior.

HANNAH'S STORY

Empty. That is the word I would use to describe my heart up until the moment I knew Jesus lived in my heart. Before Jesus, I was an anxious, lonely, people-pleasing, unmotivated, emotionally manipulative, scared, and isolated college freshman who had no idea where to turn. Being obedient to the Lord was something that confused me, and I turned my heart away from God. Little did I know God would soon change my heart.

The day Christ came into my heart began with an overcast morning on a dull Sunday. I had just woken up after a long night out and was feeling alone, regretful, and anxious. I was also feeling the heaviness of an approaching anniversary of a traumatic event in my past.

My heart was feeling alone and guarded with all kinds of emotions.

I wanted to go to church as I had in weeks past, but the friends I usually would have gone with weren't around. I wasn't ready or confident enough to go on my own, so I decided to stay home.

But God wanted me there.

He wanted me there so I could be reminded of why I am living and assured me that I don't have to navigate my life alone.

Thirty minutes before church started, a girl who I would now call a dear friend of mine texted me and asked me if I wanted to go with her to church that day. I knew it was a sign, and I had to go. God wanted me there.

Before I knew it, I was standing in church, the room filling with music and the Spirit of the Lord surrounding me. The message that day brought tears to my eyes and comfort to my aching heart about the trauma of my past and how living for the Lord can transform the way you love others and the way you love yourself.

I knew in that very moment that I was going all in. God chased after me even when I had my back turned and my identity centered around things that were temporary. I Peter 1:14 says, "As obedient children, do not conform to the evil desires you had when you lived in ignorance." Being obedient to the Lord is a life-long journey, and our paths may not look the same.

I began diving into fellowship, Bible studies, readings, and prayer. In the process, I began discovering the answers to many of the questions I'd had about Christianity for so long.

Loving the Lord with all of your heart and listening to what he has to say is hard. It takes dedication and sacrifice, and as a college girl who loved to please and be liked by others, it took a lot of commitment for me to change my heart and realize what is temporary versus what is eternal.

The Lord urged me to take a year off of school and to live at home to heal my mental health, take a break from my slipping grades, save money, and heal broken relationships. I was torn. I knew it was what was best for me, but I didn't want to lose relationships and a path of independence that I had built the year before.

After much prayer and guidance, I took the leap of faith. Now, it truly brings tears to my eyes how fruitful my life has been and how faithful God has been to my family. I can easily say that although it was hard, being obedient to the Lord has provided me with more truth, faith, hope, blessings, godly friendships, and love than I could have ever asked for. 1 John 3:24 always gives me encouragement: "The one who keeps God's commands lives in him, and he in them. And this is how we know that he lives in us: We know it by the Spirit he gave us."

Take that leap of faith and listen to the Lord with all of your heart. You never know what is around the corner. He will provide.

Read more about Abraham's story of obedience and God's faithfulness and sovereignty. Genesis 17 & Genesis 22:1-19

—————— **REFLECTION QUESTIONS** ——————

1. Why do I obey Jesus?

2. Why should I treat the Bible as an authority figure in my life?

3. Why is obedience critical in my relationship with God?

4.   What does Scripture require about obedience?

5.   Why should I listen to Scripture even if my feelings tell me otherwise?

CHAPTER 15

THEN THERE WAS ANOTHER BUTTERFLY

Remember the Why

I graduated from Colorado State University, Class of 2020. After graduation, I figured I needed to pick up a hobby before I started to lose my mind.

I chose to start walking. *A lot.*

I fell in love with putting my phone down and making it a habit to step outside every day.

When I chose to put my headphones on and turn the music up, things started changing. My creative brain started working and I felt closer to God. I started to find joy in the ordinary. Every morning I put my headphones on, stepped outside my door, and passed my favorite shops. I delighted in the smell of fresh coffee and enjoyed watching people go in and out of the different shops.

One particular morning, I was listening to a podcast episode from Red Rocks Young Adults called "The Power of Expectation." As I was listening, I was reminded of a conversation I'd had just the day before with one of my best friends. Maddie and I had been sharing deeply about the current seasons in our lives. Maddie told me that she had a deep desire to get married one day.

I didn't tell Maddie, but I had never leaned into God on this subject because I'd always been terrified of what God might tell me. I didn't want God to tell me I was called to be single my whole life. Like I said earlier, I was believing the lie that a man was the only one that would fulfill my deepest desires.

That morning, after listening to the podcast and remembering my conversation with Maddie, I began to pray as I continued walking. I told God about everything I was feeling.

I brought him my frustration and fear on this subject. I didn't know what God was promising for me in the future: singleness or marriage—both God honoring.

As I approached the top of a hill, I continued to pray to God and gave it all to him.

I told God that I put all my trust him. If he wants me to pursue singleness, I trust him in that because he knows how I am going to glorify him the most.

Something I always forget about God's character is that he cares more about our lives and knows our inmost being than we ever will (Psalm 139). My deep craving and desire for marriage is something that God has given me. He gave me a desire to want to get married for a reason. However, we are the bride of Christ. He created that desire in me to run toward Jesus. John 3:29 says "The bride belongs to the bridegroom. The friend who attends the bridegroom waits and listens for him, and is full of joy when he hears the bridegroom's voice. That joy is mine, and it is now complete."

I reached the top of the hill.

And guess what? A butterfly flew right in my face, nearly hitting me.

It flew toward some bushes. I watched and smiled because it was so pretty. It had a glow that emanated from its black-and-yellow wings.

In this small and ordinary moment, I felt a stirring in my spirit.

I knew God was telling me I needed to pay attention.

Knowing how God has used butterflies in the past to speak to me, I decided to lean in. I watched this butterfly as it was flying around bushes, smelling flowers, and pollinating nature to help the natural lifecycle. This butterfly seemed happy and focused.

Right across the way from this butterfly, I saw another butterfly going about its business too. This one seemed strong and brilliant.

They both were joyful and continued to work by themselves.

A thought came to my mind.

What if they came together? Nah, there's no freaking way will they come together.

But I knew that God was telling me to wait and watch.

I waited, probably looking like a crazy person staring at these two butterflies as people walked by. I noticed that each butterfly was doing what it was designed to do—alone. But neither seemed irritable or impatient. They were just focused on what they were supposed to do.

I, on the other hand, started feeling impatient. In fact, I started doubting God was wanting me to watch them at all. But I shifted my thoughts and reminded myself that God is full of surprises.

I kept waiting.

Sure enough, the butterfly across the way started flying in a path destined to intersect with the path of the first butterfly.

They each continued doing their own thing, but now in close proximity to each other. Then at the right time, the first butterfly came and nudged the second one.

Suddenly, they were flying together right in front of me. They joined together and continued to work and pollinate the flowers. They actually looked like they were being more effective because now they had two sets of eyes and could find pollen together easier than they could alone.

After witnessing this beautiful moment, I started crying.

I had brought my frustrations to him, and he had let me know he heard me. God knows the longings of my heart.

I felt that through these butterflies, God was speaking to me the purpose of marriage. The purpose of marriage is to have your own personal relationship with Jesus and to focus on your ministry. Then if it's in God's will, he will bring you someone that is doing the exact same thing to make his ministry effective and God honoring too. All the while, pushing each other toward Jesus and knowing the true love of God. Whatever God has for me, I am content with Jesus. With Jesus, that joy is made complete. Jesus is the ultimate love story. We are his bride. God made a covenant through Jesus to allow us to have a sacrificial love and bring us into a beautiful union. A marriage here on earth means joining hands with a missionary partner who points to Jesus. When we die, we will not be married as referred to in Luke 20:35.

As I continued to walk, a huge monarch butterfly flew across my path. It looked just like the butterfly that had flown in my face several years earlier when I had been in a completely different season of life.

Right then, God reminded me of how much I have grown and how much God has brought me through. I started praising God for this incredible moment. How cool is God that he speaks to us in ways that not only meet our needs and desires but are unique to our hearts?

I have an app called the *Sprinkle of Jesus*. It has been a game changer. It's an app that encourages you and gives you a notification each day to continue to be reminded of Jesus. When I was almost done with my walk, I got the "sprinkle" for the day: "Don't rush God's promise. The process is important before you get to the promise." What a beautiful reminder to be content in singleness and to focus on my pursuit of Jesus while continuing to work on my purpose and dreams in life. God promises us that Jesus is coming back for us and that we will spend eternity with him.

The importance of reminding yourself *why* you are pursuing Jesus is a constant battle. It doesn't come overnight, and it for sure doesn't last if you're not continuing to put effort into renewing your heart and mind (Romans 12:2).

There is so much to cover, and there are only so many words I can put down on every page without making you fall asleep and wanting to put this book down. "So I will always remind you of these things, even though you know them and are firmly established in the truth you now have" (2 Peter 1:12).

Remember your why.

Why are you pursuing purity?
Why are you persevering when life is hard?
Why are you choosing joy?
Why are you following Jesus?
Why is forgiveness important?
Why is loving yourself and finding your identity in Christ important?

Remind yourself of these things.

WHY DO *YOU* FOLLOW JESUS?

"I follow Jesus because I am a better person when I pursue his love. I turn to him in everything. I was always raised in the Christian faith, but now I have made the decision to continue to walk in my faith, and I am proud of that."

—Tessa

"I follow Jesus because he has saved me from the emptiness I felt in my life. He has given me a purpose on earth I couldn't see for myself."

—Sarah

"I follow Jesus because his unconditional love has completely changed my life and the person I am today. He offered me freedom from the purposeless life I was living and showed me a path to the important things to strive for in life."

—Caroline

"I follow Jesus because he died to give me life. He is worthy of more than I could ever give back to Him."

—Makayla

"I continue to follow Jesus because everything that I have ever wanted, I find and continue to find in Jesus.

It's the comfort of knowing that I don't have to have it all together to come before him or even know what to do next. But I do know that when I put my trust in Jesus, I don't ever have to fear being let down. I know and stand on the truth that whatever he has planned for me is better than what I can do or what the world could ever give me. I rely on the truth that he will always love me, that I will never have to work for his approval to accept me, and that I am worth it. It's the little things to why I will continue to follow Jesus the rest of my days."

—Nya

"I follow Jesus because he is truth. The things that surround us on earth lead us to believe so many lies about our identity, worth, and expectations. Jesus grounds me and affirms that (even to a power as great as he) I am invaluable."

—Leigh

"I follow Jesus because he gave his life for me to be renewed, to be truly loved, and to become a citizen of heaven. Because his ways are better than mine, I choose to take up my cross and walk with him every day."

—Macie

"I follow Jesus because I am helpless in this world and in need of a Savior. Everything else in this lifetime only offers temporary satisfaction disguised with temporary pleasure. Jesus is truly everlasting."

—Emily

"I follow Jesus for many reasons. We are not meant to go through this life alone, and Jesus is the only one that you can always count on to be there, no matter what else happens in this crazy world. I've also seen firsthand what a kind, loving, and selfless woman my mom is because of her love for Jesus, and I aspire to be more like her in every way that I can."

—Kate

"I am beginning to follow Jesus because the peace I have felt from beginning to trust that someone loves and cares about my story and plans has been more comforting than anything I can remember in my life. I am beginning to see things in a positive light by remembering to thank God for the little things rather than ruminating on the bad things—even though it's easier to sometimes be negative."

—Kathryn

"Why do I follow Jesus? When I feel like no one understands and feels what I am going through, I am reminded of the God who became human to feel what I am feeling. He was immersed in pain, hurt, and sadness in order to love us better. Who else would intentionally go through that pain for me?"

—Lexine

"I follow Jesus because he embodies love as an action and dismantles oppressive systems of injustice in the same way that I hope to with my life."

—Bella

"I follow Jesus because he is the only way. I have often strayed down so many troublesome paths, and he is the only one waiting for me at the end. Jesus knows the best way, and having him in my life and pushing to follow that way is what brings me hope. He has made his mark on my life through only the work God can do; therefore, I will spend the rest of my life chasing him."

—Rachel

"I follow Jesus because I know that I am protected and loved at all times. The relationship that a person can build with Jesus is so important because not only do you build trust with him, but you build trust with yourself and find out more about yourself that you didn't know before. I also think that being able to always come back to Jesus in any time of need/struggle has been so beneficial to me as I follow and learn more about him."

—Addison

"I follow Jesus because he has felt so close and real to me during some of my lowest and loneliest times. I have felt so overwhelmed by his presence and love for me that there is no way I could ever doubt his existence."

—Shantel

"I follow Jesus because he has constantly pursued me my whole life. Through nature, music, people, or events, Jesus continuously attempts to capture my heart."

—Carly

"I follow Jesus because for the first time since accepting him into my life, I feel fully known, and one of my biggest fears is not being fully known. Following Jesus keeps me grounded and constantly reminds me of my worth. I have a lot of inner demons, but it's cool to know that Jesus loves me as I am and my identity is totally secure and found in Christ."

—Taylor

"I follow Jesus because he makes me feel known and pursues me each and every single day. He doesn't stop pursing me."

—Sally

"I follow Jesus because he is the Redeemer who is constant and simply too good not to believe."

—Emma

Now that you have finished this book, write your own why! I follow Jesus because . . .

RESOURCES AND RECOMMENDED READING

For relationships and singleness:
- *Relationship Goals* by Michael Todd
- *Loving Your Husband Before You Have One* by Kim Vollendorf

For the power of prayer:
- *Dangerous Prayers* by Craig Groeschel
- *The Circle Maker* by Mark Batterson

For finding your purpose:
- *The Road Back to You: An Enneagram Journey to Self-Discovery* by Ian Morgan Cron and Suzanne Stabile
- *Unsatisfied* by Sean Vollendorf

For learning to love yourself and diving deeper in your past:
- *Uninvited: Living Loved When You Feel Less Than, Left Out and Lonely* by Lysa Terkeust
- *Lies Women Believe* by Nancy Leigh DeMoss
- *Emotionally Healthy Spirituality* by Peter and Geri Scazzero

- *Emotionally Healthy Leader* by Peter Scazzero
- *Emotionally Healthy Relationships* by Peter Scazzero
- *What's Your Secret?* By Aaron Stern
- *Love Secrets* by John Mark Pantana
- *In his Image* by Jen Wilkin

For surrendering control in your finances:
- *The Total Money Makeover* by Dave Ramsey

For the spiritual world and heaven:
- *Heaven and Back* by Mary C. Neal

For truth and grace:
- *Crazy Love* by Francis Chan

For rest:
- *The Ruthless Elimination* of Hurry by John Mark Comer

For discipline:
- *Atomic Habits* by James Clear
- *The Deeply Formed Life* by Rich Villodas
- *Essentialism: The Disciplined Pursuit of Less* by Greg McKeown

For loving others:

- *Love Does* by Bob Goff
- *The Gospel Comes with a House Key* by Rosaria Butterfield

For theology:

- *Surprised by Hope: Rethinking Heaven, the Resurrection, and the Mission of the Church* by N.T. Wright
- *Mere Christianity* by C.S. Lewis
- *The Case for Christ* by Lee Strobel

For hearing God:

- *Hearing God* by Dallas Willard

For Racial Reconciliation:

- *Be the Bridge* by Latasha Morrison

ABOUT THE AUTHOR

$\mathcal{L}$indsea Pattison found herself frustrated while following Jesus. She needed a continuous reminder of why she started pursuing him in the first place.

She had to go back and remind herself to fall in love with Jesus. Finding the answer to her searching questions motivated her to open her laptop in a local coffee shop and write to young women feeling the same way.

Lindsea is an up-and-coming author, content creator, and cookie lover. She graduated from Colorado State University with a Bachelor of Liberal Arts, studying journalism and media communications.

She has a passion for sharing the love of Jesus with high school and college women. Her dream is to pursue documentary film in the hope of spreading the gospel overseas and to the lost.

To those who know her best, Lindsea is an imperfect lover of Jesus found typically somewhere outside in nature or on a couch writing in her journal wrapped in a cozy blanket and drinking tea.

Share your story with me on my website, through a DM or by an email.

Website: Lindseapattison.com

Instagram: @rememberthewhybook

Contact: lindseapattison@gmail.com